CAKE
magic

First published in the United Kingdom in 2011 by
Pavilion Books
Old West London Magistrates Court
10 Southcombe Street
London, W14 0RA

An imprint of Anova Books Company Ltd

Associate Publisher: Nina Sharman
Copy editor: Diana Vowles
Proofreader: Julia Halford
Designer: Ros Saunders
Home economist: Kate Shirazi
Photographer: Emma Solley

ISBN 978-1-86205-9177

A CIP catalogue record for this book is available from the British Library.

10 9 8 7 6 5 4 3 2 1

Reproduction by Dot Gradations Ltd, UK
Printed and bound by Everbest Printing Ltd., China

www.anovabooks.com

Kate Shirazi

CAKE
magic

PAVILION

Contents

Introduction

I am a very greedy person. Even when I'm not actually eating I'm generally thinking about food, and cakes are a particular culinary fascination of mine.

I'm not sure why, but it may have something to do with their being one of life's 'extras'. Cake doesn't really feature very highly on Maslow's hierarchy of needs. Shelter? Tick. Safe and warm? Tick. Cake? Study it as I may, I can't find a mention of cake anywhere, though I feel hopeful that if the great man had expanded on physiological needs and food in general he may have muttered about a small slice of something being particularly helpful. Well, I am here to fly the flag for cake.

We're constantly bombarded these days by two messages. First, everything must be done very, very quickly. Cook an interesting and delicious supper in 10 minutes; organize your winter wardrobe at the press of a button; master the intricacies of DNA sequencing before the sun is over the yard arm. Secondly, all morsels that pass our lips should be without added sugar, fat, flour or generally anything that goes into a cake. Oh dear. I would like to live to a ripe old age. I don't want to be morbidly obese, or riddled with diabetic complications. But I also don't want to live on a diet of mung beans, windfall apples and a spot of marinated tofu for the rest of my life. I truly believe in following a balanced diet. Don't cut out anything completely, just go easy on the stuff you know isn't top of the health-giving list (for instance, cakes and chips – yum). Can we just get back to being sensible? Please? At the time of writing, I'm a normal size and in rude health. I eat cake most days, which I admit is probably too often, but I do only eat a small amount. And I exercise. And I eat a balanced diet. It seems to work. Amazing. In fact, hold the front page: 'Woman does not overeat or under eat and remains healthily between size 10 and 12 depending on what shop she is in.' Extraordinary.

I have now finished ranting about diet and will rant instead about time. Brace yourselves. Speed is not always of the essence. Yes, you can whip up a baked delight and have it out of the oven in under 30 minutes (cupcakes, Victoria sponge, scones and so on), but do not ignore the joy of a boiled fruit cake that fills your house with the spicy, fruity scents of your labours. Or perhaps a yeast-based slab of warm, comforting, soft, sweet tea bread – or a baked doughnut fresh out of the oven, with its sticky, sugary coating and blob of hot, oozy jam. The truth is that most of the recipes that look like a day's hard graft usually have only about 30 minutes of actual hands-on faff time. The rest of the time is spent online shopping for shoes, googling George Clooney, and wondering about sneaking in a bit of a lie-down while the dough does its thing. True enough, there are long-winded recipes in this book, too. I cannot lie. These are for when you want to embrace the afternoon and devote yourself to some very finely tuned faffing. Basically, what I'm saying is that there is a cake for every occasion and for every level of time constraint, budget and faff – or lack of it.

While we're on the subject of occasion and cake, can you tell me when an occasion is not appropriate to wheel out a small slither of something? True, the cake needs to be chosen carefully; there's no point in giving the fine ladies of an upmarket part of town a wodge of farmer's boiled fruit cake, nor would a morsel of their flourless hazelnut sponge go down too well in the cab of a tractor, what with all the mucking about with plates and forks and so on. But place a cake in someone's line of vision and they cannot ignore it. A little sparkle appears in their eyes. In fact, it doesn't even need to be a real cake – a picture does it. I'll bet you've already had a sneaky peek at the pictures in this book and earmarked which ones you want to have a go at, based purely on your emotional response to a glimpse of a picture.

Giving someone a cake as a present is a truly lovely thing to do. If someone has just moved house, flowers are gorgeous and add a certain sense of civility to the surrounding chaos – if you can find a vase. But the sight of a tin (pan) or Tupperware box containing a whole cake brings tears to the eyes. I would stipulate that a moving-in cake really should come from the 'everyday' section; nothing too showy-offy or elaborate that boasts about your own kitchen being all unpacked and ordered. Don't rub it in. A good old Victoria sponge or an honest ginger cake hits the spot perfectly.

If someone needs cheering up, take them a cake. I'm really not being flippant here, but in the worst-case scenarios that life chucks at us, a quiet gift of a cake is like giving someone a huge hug. It lets them know that you love them enough to invest your time and energy in creating something to nourish them physically and emotionally. Or maybe you've just started a new romance and don't know what to do? Still in that awkward fancy-them-so-much-it-hurts-but-don't-want-to-freak-them-out stage? Bake them a cake. Honestly – good results in the romance stakes are guaranteed. You'll see.

So you will now realize, dear readers, that cakes are a highly appropriate part of everyone's diet. Marie Antoinette may have had a point. The time has come to stop wittering about the marvels of the stuff and get down to the nitty-gritty of equipment and ingredients. Plus, of course, what can go wrong and why, and how to resolve the situation without throwing a massive tantrum and getting yourself into an unnecessary state. It's not attractive.

Those of you who are familiar with my style of cooking know that I am a 'fling it in and see what happens' kind of cook. However, may I reassure you that the recipes contained in this book have actually been made, and I carefully wrote down what I chucked in, and how much of it there was. So you can be confident that the recipes work and are not just the ravings of a woman who hasn't even had the sense to see if they are edible – but if you like to take the free-fall approach, go for it! Swap ingredients around, add new flavours and bake in different ways. Use the recipes as a starting point and fly by the seat of your pants. Having said that, when I am baking, I measure ingredients far more than when I am cooking something savoury, since the proportions of fat to flour and egg need to be in the right vicinity if a cake is going to cook properly and have a pleasing texture. I do, however, constantly change the type of dried fruit, flavourings and shape of tin (pan).

The outs and ins of tins (pans)

Tins are an interesting thing in baking. Bear with me, they are. For a long time I possessed only two baking tins – one of which was actually a small roasting tin. They did me proud. Of course, when a recipe stated that I must use a 20 cm/8 in loose-bottomed tin, I stared at my choice of two, neither of which could be described as 20 cm/8 in or even perfectly round (there was a dropping incident) and each of which had a bottom that was definitely fixed. So, I had educated guesses to make.

This general lack of receptacles taught me some valuable lessons; first, if you have the stated tin, why not use it? But if you haven't, don't panic. Choose the tin that is nearest to the size and make allowances for cooking times. A cake mixture that goes into a smaller tin will take longer to cook. The top may have cremated itself before the middle is done, so you will need to cover it with greaseproof paper (parchment paper) when it starts to look as if it might go horribly wrong. Then it can sit happily for the rest of the cooking time without the top going black. A cake tin that is bigger than suggested in the recipe will result in a flatter cake that will need less cooking time. It's not rocket science. If a recipe asks for two or three sandwich tins, but you've only got one deep round tin, bung it all in and split the cake into three when it is cooked. Only got a round tin and recipe wants square? Shout at the book 'I will not have square cakes in this house!' and put it in the round tin. There will be no knock on the door as the cake-shape police come storming into the kitchen to monitor the situation.

Loose-bottomed tins are useful devils, as are springform tins (especially for cheesecakes). If you're serious about cake-making, it might be worth investing in a range of different-sized round tins, a square tin and a loaf tin. However, I don't want you to start spending loads of money on tins you'll never use, so decide what works best for you. I love a heavy non-stick tin, but, again, it's your choice.

You'll notice that loads of the recipes ask you to 'grease and line the tin'. At the risk of teaching my grandmother to suck eggs, I shall go through this now. Tins (even the non-stick ones) need to be prepared properly before you bung the mixture in if you ever want your cake to come out in one piece. Grease the tin first with a dab of butter or margarine, then pop the tin on top of some greaseproof paper and draw round it. Cut out the base and put it to one side. Cut a strip of greaseproof paper into a rectangle as long as the circumference of the tin and 2 cm/¾ in higher than the depth. Fold the 2 cm/¾ in strip upwards and make small snips every 2 cm/¾ in or so up to the fold line. Place the rectangle inside the tin – the cut bits should happily sit along the base of the tin and the paper should stick to the greased sides. Then pop the base piece on top.

So, you've lined your tin (which may or may not be of the appropriate size). Now for the mixing. A wooden spoon and a valiant thrashing using good old elbow grease are fine up to a point. You are letting yourself in for a workout here and are committing to expending some serious effort. If you're not prepared to work up a sweat, may I suggest the interference of a little electricity? I am a huge fan of the upright mixer. In my world, they cannot be, er, beaten. If you don't have a mixer a food processor works quite well, even though it chops rather than beats. A handheld electric whisk is also useful and I would always choose one of these alternatives over reliance on my delicate arms, a wooden spoon and a lazy nature.

Basic ingredients

Hens are extremely good to us. They lay their eggs and don't make a fuss about it. They don't bite (no teeth), don't howl at the moon, don't go on the rampage scaring old ladies and young children, and don't sit on low walls flicking lit cigarettes at passersby. And what do we do? Cram them into metal cages all piled on top of each other in what I think of as warehouses of doom; then, when they are about 18 months old, ship them off to the fast-food factory. Chicken nugget, anyone? Down the hill from my home is a free-range hen operation. Hundreds and hundreds of brown fluffy-bottomed girls can be seen going about their business (hens are generally very busy creatures), gossiping and scratching around and being naturally hen-like. If people could see the difference between the production of eggs from caged hens and free-range hens, I really think they wouldn't be so drawn to the 'value' eggs. My message is simple: buy free-range eggs or I will train hens to sit on a low wall near you and start flicking lit cigarettes.

On to less aggressive tactics now, but a no less thorny subject, it would appear: butter versus margarine. Butter is heavenly in a cake, and a lot of these recipes stipulate butter in the ingredients list. But I really and truly believe that not all margarine is bad margarine, and some of the recipes use a soft type – a good-quality one does not contain any hydrogenated fat, trans fatty acids or any of the other scary nasties found in cheap margarines. The other thing in their favour is that the good ones often contain buttermilk, which is excellent for flavour and texture in a cake. An all-in-one sponge (one of my all-time useful and favourite baking methods) calls for soft margarine. It simply doesn't work well with butter, even if you have softened it.

So please don't disregard a recipe because it uses margarine – use butter if you really want to, but the texture and flavour of the cake will not be how it was intended. (However, if you love it – fantastic!) Sometimes butter is an absolute must: buttercream is not good with margarine. Not good at all. In fact, bad. So all in all, up to you, but whatever the recipe uses, this works and I cannot vouch for substitutions!

Cocoa is not the same as drinking chocolate, and if you choose to cook with drinking chocolate instead of cocoa, the result will be fairly grim. Just compare the ingredients list on the tins if you don't believe me. No recipe in this book calls for drinking chocolate. Leave the tin alone.

Timing and testing

Ovens and their vagaries are always a bit of a nightmare when it comes to writing recipes. Even if we all had the same make and model of oven, I would bet that they would all cook slightly differently. So, bearing in mind that some of us have fan ovens, some have gas, some have Agas, some have snazzy and some have basic, there is no way that if a recipe says 'bakes in 20 minutes' you can take that as the law. I have had an oven where the far left cooked at about three times the rate of the near right – which meant the palaver of turning things 90 degrees at various points in the cooking. You know your cooker. Have a peep at the cake at least 5 minutes before the end of the allotted time and see whether it's time to a) retrieve it; b) cover it with a bit of greaseproof paper to prevent the top burning and give it another 10 minutes; or c) just to leave it another 5 minutes. It's a judgment call – yours. A cake is generally done when a sharp knife or skewer stuck into it comes back clean without any globs of raw cake mixture sticking to it. It should be firm to the touch, and in the case of a sponge, have a bit of a spring to it when you give it a mild poke. Finger sinking into the midst – not good. Being able to rap your knuckles on the top of a carbonated surface – also not good.

Troubleshooting

So, you've followed all the instructions and something has still gone wrong. Here follows a small compendium of what might have caused the problem and, ultimately, how to wriggle your way out of it. If your cake is solid and brick-like, it might be for a couple of reasons: you may not have beaten enough air into the mixture (did you use a wooden spoon and come over all weak?), or if the recipe required you to fold in the flour, you may have been a bit too vigorous and bashed all the air out of your mixture. Did you use butter in an all-in-one recipe? I don't want to say 'I told you so', but really ...

* If your cake is a bit dry and crumbly, the mixture might have been too stiff and dry and the oven temperature may have been a little on the high side. Next time, lower the oven temperature and add a splash of milk to the batter.
* If the fruit sinks to the bottom of your cake, it's generally because it's too damp or sticky. I always rinse and dry glacé (candied) cherries. The mixture may have been a bit too soft to carry the fruit as it rises.
* A cake that's sinking in the middle may be due to a couple of reasons: there may have been too much raising agent, or too soft a mixture. Check the oven temperature, too. An oven that is too hot or too cool can cause a cake to sink.
* Don't chuck out a cake because of its texture. If it is inedible as a cake, make it into cake crumbs and freeze them – there are loads of uses for cake crumbs in other recipes and it's handy to have a stash tucked away. If the cake is flat and tragic, use a cutter to cut out shapes and sandwich them together with jam or buttercream.
* With a cake that has risen unevenly, just level the top, turn it upside down and ice the bottom.
* A cake with a massively sunken middle can be turned into a mega pudding; cut out the centre and pile whipped cream and fruit into the hole. A dusting of icing (confectioners') sugar, and voilà!

Never admit that the cake you present with a flourish is not what you had first envisaged. A cake is a wonderful thing, full stop. No one need ever know, and only a very mean-spirited person would comment negatively about a cake that someone else has made. In fact, take the cake away from them – they don't deserve it. They can watch other people eat it. That'll teach them.

Now, stop all this reading and go and bake!

Everyday cakes

By everyday cakes, I mean cakes that are fairly quick and simple – something to put into the cake tin (pan). A cake that's not going to set the world on fire, but it will be delicious and will certainly fill a cake-shaped hole in your tummy. Everyday cakes shouldn't be stressful to either bake or eat. I think of them as 'honest' cakes; they don't require an extensive list of ingredients, a complicated method or specialist equipment. Some are sponge-based and some are denser, fruit-packed numbers. I think that there should really be an everyday cake to suit most moods and weather conditions – doesn't a bleak wintery day shout 'fruitcake' at you? Is it just me? Oh. OK, then. In my world, a summer's day calls for a lovely light orange and lemon sponge and autumn definitely means apple and ginger. These are cakes that don't require much thought, but when you need to get a cake in the oven quick sharp, you have the ingredients to hand.

You may notice that chocolate doesn't feature very highly in this chapter. When I was writing the recipes it struck me that, apart from your basic chocolate sponge sandwich, most other chocolate cakes are rather fancy-schmancy numbers. I am not knocking these; believe me, the posh cake chapter is crammed to the gunwales with them. My husband rather wistfully asked for a chocolate orange cake one day. Feeling rather guilty for not asking him earlier if he had any special cake requests, I knocked up the chocolate orange loaf. Really easy and definitely one for the everyday section.

Quite a few of these recipes feature dried fruit. If you are wary of the fruit-sinking issue, please see the nugget in the Introduction about fruit-sink prevention (p.15).

The vast majority of these cakes are really good keepers – that is, they either mature (ginger, apple and banana cakes are all excellent after a few days) or sit very happily in a tin for about a week without any sign of sulking or drying out. All in all, these are your reliable best friends in the cake world. Not too good looking, not too clever, just always fun to be around and always delicious.

Victoria sponge

Aaah. The mother of all everyday cakes. It is like the comforting, delicious faithful friend of the cake world. The house smells gorgeous when it's in the oven, it's a doddle to make and you can vary it by changing the jam in the middle, adding buttercream, fresh cream, luscious strawberries or raspberries when they are at their best – the possibilities are endless. Victoria sponge, we salute you.

✳ Serves 8

175 g/6 oz/1 ½ cups
    self-raising flour, sifted

175 g/6 oz/¾ cup caster
    (superfine) sugar

175 g/6 oz/¾ cup soft margarine

3 large free-range eggs

1 tsp vanilla extract

1 tbsp strawberry jam

icing (confectioners') sugar
    for dusting

Preheat the oven to 160°C/325°F/Gas mark 3. Grease and line two 20 cm/8 in round sandwich tins (pans). Put all the ingredients except the jam and the icing (confectioners') sugar in a large bowl and beat the living daylights out of them. The preferred method is in a freestanding mixer, but you could use an electric hand whisk.

When the mixture is very pale, fluffy and almost mousse-like, divide it between the prepared tins and smooth out. Bake for about 20 minutes. The cakes should be springy to the touch and a skewer or sharp knife should come out clean when poked into the sponge.

Cool the cakes on a wire rack. When they are cold, sandwich them together with the jam, and dust the top with icing sugar. Voilà!

Everyday coffee cake

I love coffee cake. So scrumptious. The key is to add enough coffee.
If you're going to have coffee cake, it really should taste of coffee, don't
you think? The walnuts on top are optional – as is the icing. You could
increase the amount of buttercream and put that on top of the cake,
if you wish. Alternatively, leave it naked. Radical.

✳ Serves 8

175 g/6 oz/1 ½ cups self-raising flour, sifted

175 g/6 oz/¾ cup caster (superfine) sugar

175 g/6 oz/¾ cup soft margarine

3 large free-range eggs

8 heaped tsp instant coffee granules

75 g/2 ½ oz/¼ cup plus 1 tbsp unsalted butter

300 g/10 oz/2 cups icing (confectioners') sugar, sifted

8 walnut halves

Preheat the oven to 160°C/325°F/Gas mark 3. Grease and line two 20 cm/8 in round sandwich tins (pans). In a mixer, beat together the flour, caster (superfine) sugar, margarine and eggs until they are very pale and fluffy.

Put the coffee granules in a cup or small bowl and add about 3 teaspoons boiling water. The coffee should be very, very dark and just runny – if it's a bit stiff, add a few drops more water, but it certainly shouldn't look like ordinary coffee. You want a liquor that will give a huge hit of coffee without having to add too much volume of liquid.

Add 1 teaspoon coffee mixture to the cake mix and beat it in. Have a taste, and add more coffee if you think it needs it. Don't throw away any remaining mixture!

Divide the mixture between the two tins and smooth out. Bake for about 20 minutes until the cakes are firm and springy to the touch. Cool the cakes on a wire rack while you crack on with the filling and icing.

Beat the butter and 150 g/5 oz/1 cup plus 2 tbsp icing (confectioners') sugar together until pale and soft. Add 1 teaspoon coffee mixture and taste. If the balance is fine, leave it there, but you may wish to add a little more.

In another bowl, add the remaining coffee mixture to the remaining icing sugar and mix until you have a smooth mixture with the consistency of custard. If it's too runny, add more icing sugar; if too thick, add a drop of water.

When the sponges are cold, sandwich them together with the buttercream and then ice the top of the cake with the coffee icing. Place the walnuts around the edge of the cake and leave the icing to set, which should only take about an hour or so.

Lemon drizzle

There are so many variations of lemon drizzle that I have decided not to be a smartypants and try to reinvent the wheel. This is my friend Helen's lemon drizzle recipe. I have eaten it many times – it's a good 'un. The other great thing is that this recipe makes two – one for now and one for the freezer. Genius.

* Makes 2 x 450 g/1 lb loaves

100 g/3½ oz/scant ½ cup soft margarine

175 g/6 oz/1 ½ cups self-raising flour, sifted

175 g/6 oz/¾ cup caster (superfine) sugar

2 large free-range eggs

4 tbsp milk

grated zest and juice of 2 unwaxed lemons

100 g/3 ½ oz/½ cup granulated sugar

Preheat the oven to 160°C/325°F/Gas mark 3. Grease and line two 450 g/1 lb loaf tins (pans). Put the margarine, flour, caster (superfine) sugar, eggs, milk and lemon zest into a large bowl or mixer and beat away until the mixture is really pale and fluffy. Divide the mixture between the two tins and smooth the surfaces. Bake for about 30 minutes, or until the cakes are firm and springy to the touch and a knife or skewer comes out clean.

Mix the lemon juice and granulated sugar in a bowl and as soon as the cakes come out of the oven, spread this mixture over the surface of both cakes. Leave the cakes to cool in their tins while they absorb the gorgeous lemony-sugary topping. Turn them out of the tins when they are completely cold.

Gretchen's ginger cake

Wonder-cook Gretchen gave me this recipe. It's a winner. The icing is an amazing addition which I implore you not to neglect. Thanks, Gretch!

✳ Serves 10

225 g/8 oz/2 cups self-raising
  flour, sifted

1 tsp bicarbonate of soda
  (baking soda)

1 tbsp ground ginger

1 tsp mixed spice

1 tsp ground cinnamon

110 g/4 oz/½ cup cold unsalted
  butter, cubed

100 g/3 ½ oz/1 cup crystallized
  (candied) stem ginger,
  finely chopped

110 g/4 oz/⅔ cup dark
  muscovado sugar

110 g/4 oz/¼ cup black treacle

110 g/4 oz/¼ cup golden syrup

250 ml/8 fl oz/1 cup milk

1 large free-range egg

50 g/1 ¾ oz/⅓ cup icing
  (confectioners') sugar, sifted

zest of ½ lemon

zest of ½ orange

1 tbsp lemon or orange juice

Preheat the oven to 160°C/325°F/Gas mark 3. Grease and line an 18 cm/7 in round cake tin (pan) – preferably loose-bottomed or springform. In a large bowl, mix together the flour, bicarbonate of soda (baking soda) and spices. Add the butter and rub it into the dry mixture until you have a consistency like dry breadcrumbs. Add the stem ginger and stir it in.

Put the sugar, treacle, syrup and milk into a pan and gently heat until the sugar has dissolved. Turn up the heat and bring to a simmer, then take the pan off the heat and let it cool slightly. Once it has cooled down, add it to the flour mixture, stirring as you pour. Finally, stir in the egg. Pour the mixture into the tin and bake for 50–60 minutes or until a knife or skewer poked in comes out clean.

Leave the cake to cool completely in the tin and crack on with the icing. Just combine the icing (confectioners') sugar and citrus zest and juice until you have a quite thin, runny icing. Drizzle over the ginger cake and leave to set. Just delicious.

Basic chocolate cake

OK, calling a chocolate cake 'basic' might be a bit off-putting, but this is a no-nonsense chocolate sponge sandwich. It is what it is. There's no getting away from it, but it's a cake that is ultimately very yummy and very few people will turn their noses up at the offer of a slice.

The crucial thing that makes this cake great rather than OK is the quality of the cocoa you use. Do not, under any circumstances, use drinking chocolate. Not all cocoa powders are equal, either. I favour Green & Blacks. I think it gives a really rich, smooth flavour to the cake, but, of course, it's your choice.

✳ Serves 8

150 g/5 oz/1 ⅓ cups self-raising flour, sifted

175 g/6 oz/¾ cup caster (superfine) sugar

175 g/6 oz/¾ cup soft margarine

3 large free-range eggs

1 tbsp milk

50 g/1 ¾ oz/scant ½ cup cocoa powder, sifted

100 g/3 ½ oz/scant ½ cup unsalted butter

200 g/7 oz/1 ⅓ cups icing (confectioners') sugar, sifted

1–2 tsp milk (optional)

chocolate buttons, to decorate (optional)

Preheat the oven to 160°C/325°F/Gas mark 3. Grease and line two 20 cm/8 in round sandwich tins (pans). In a mixer (preferably), beat together the flour, caster (superfine) sugar, margarine, eggs, milk and half the cocoa powder. Beat for about 2 minutes until the mixture is pale brown and fluffy. Divide between the two tins and smooth the surfaces. Bake for about 20 minutes or until the tops of the cakes are firm and springy to the touch. Turn out the cakes onto wire racks to cool.

While the cakes are cooling, make the buttercream. Beat together the butter, icing (confectioners') sugar and remaining cocoa until soft and fluffy. If necessary, add a teaspoon or so of milk to get a softer consistency – you need to be able to spread this.

When the cakes are cold, sandwich them together with half the buttercream and spread the remaining buttercream on the top of the cake. Decorate, if you wish, with chocolate buttons or any other chocolate that takes your fancy.

Easy fruit cake

I am a bit wary of fruit cakes. The term covers those dark, dry numbers with a bit of marzipan and rock-hard icing that lie in sad little fingers on a tray, getting drier and drier and sadder and sadder. A bad fruit cake is a depressing, soul-destroying affair. A good fruit cake is a wonderful, life-affirming experience that makes you savour the juiciness and richness – and that's even without the addition of a little alcohol. This is a recipe for a boiled fruit cake – the stuff of everyday.

✳ Serves 8–10

110 g/4 oz/⅔ cup raisins

110 g/4 oz/⅔ cup ready-to-eat dried apricots

50 g/1 ¾ oz/⅓ cup dried cherries

110 g/4 oz/⅔ cup dried peaches (or pears)

150 ml/5 fl oz/⅔ cup water

110 g/4 oz/½ cup unsalted butter

110 g/4 oz/⅔ cup dark muscovado sugar

2 large free-range eggs, beaten

1 tsp mixed spice

225 g/8 oz/2 cups self-raising flour, sifted

Preheat the oven to 150°C/300°F/Gas mark 2. Grease and line a 20 cm/8 in cake tin (pan). Put the dried fruit, water, butter and sugar into a saucepan and heat gently until the mixture comes up to simmering point. Simmer for about 20 minutes, giving it a stir every now and again to stop the mixture sticking.

Let the mixture cool for a while – if you add the eggs while it's too hot you get scrambled eggs. When it's cool, add the eggs and spice and sift the flour over the top of it all. Mix it all up well – and this is where you really don't need a mixer; a wooden spoon is perfect.

Tip the mixture into the tin and smooth the top. I like to make a little indent in the centre of the cake as I think it helps to prevent it doming. Bake for about 1 ½ hours, checking after an hour to see if it's done by sticking a knife or a skewer in to see if it comes out clean. If it needs longer in the oven and the top is getting a bit too brown, cover it in greaseproof paper (parchment paper).

Let the cake cool in the tin for about 20 minutes before turning out onto a wire rack to cool.

Carrot cake

I make this in a square tin, but there is absolutely no reason why you have to. This is a recipe that positively welcomes additions: raisins, orange zest, chopped nuts, different spices or toppings all work really well. View this as a base carrot cake recipe and make it your own – indeed, it need never be the same twice.

✳ Serves 8-10

175 ml/6 fl oz/¾ cup sunflower oil

175 g/6 oz/1 cup soft light brown sugar

3 large free-range eggs

150 g/5 oz/1 ⅓ cups plain (all-purpose) flour

1 ½ tsp bicarbonate of soda (baking soda)

1 ½ tsp baking powder

1 tsp ground cinnamon

225 g/8 oz/1 ¼ cups grated carrot

25 g/1 oz/1 ¾ tbsp unsalted butter

200 g/7 oz/1 ¼ cups icing (confectioners') sugar, sifted

25 g/1 oz/1 ¾ tbsp cream cheese

Preheat the oven to 180°C/350°F/Gas mark 4. Grease and line a 20 cm/8 in square tin (pan). In a large bowl, whisk together the oil and the brown sugar, then add the eggs and whisk away. Sift in the flour, bicarbonate of soda (baking soda), baking powder and cinnamon and whisk some more. When everything is fully whisked, stir in the grated carrot. Pour the mixture into the tin and bake for 20-25 minutes until the top is springy and an inserted knife or skewer comes out clean. Cool the cake in its tin for 10 minutes before turning it onto a wire rack to become completely cold.

Meanwhile, make the icing. Cream together the butter and icing (confectioners') sugar until well incorporated and the butter has really softened. The mixture should be really quite stiff. Then carefully work in the cream cheese – don't overdo it, because it can make the topping go really runny. If it gets too thin, just add more icing sugar until you obtain the consistency you are after. Add any flavouring you like at this stage: orange juice or zest, a smidge of honey, vanilla – anything that takes your fancy. Spread the icing over the cake and scoff.

Apple crumble cake

I would just like you to know that I had a couple of humdinger failures writing this recipe. I thought it might cheer you. Imagine a cake where the crumble has sunk into the sponge as it has cooked, displacing the apple and settling in a cement-like wodge of unpleasantness. Now that was a cake that really couldn't be rescued. This, however, is the phoenix that has risen from the apple-cement-gloop ashes. I proudly present to you a wonder of a cake that is delicious cold with a cup of tea, or warm with a dollop of cream.

✳ Serves 8–10

75g/2 ½ oz/¼ cup plus 1 tbsp unsalted butter

75 g/2 ½ oz/¾ cup plain (all-purpose) flour, sifted

100 g/3 ½ oz/scant ½ cup caster (superfine) sugar

110 g/4 oz/1 cup self-raising flour, sifted

1 large free-range egg

2 tsp ground cinnamon

2 tbsp milk

4 large dessert apples such as Braeburn, peeled, cored and thinly sliced

2 tbsp demerara sugar

Preheat the oven to 160°C/325°F/Gas mark 3. Grease and line a deep 20 cm/8 in loose-bottomed round tin (pan). Loose-bottomed makes all the difference here, believe me.

Make the crumble mixture by rubbing 25 g/1 oz/1 ¾ tbsp butter into the plain (all-purpose) flour and then adding 50 g/1 ¾ oz/scant ¼ cup caster (superfine) sugar. Sprinkle over about 1 tablespoon water and, with a fork, turn it over a bit so you have a clumpy type of crumble mix.

Place the self-raising flour, the remaining butter and sugar, the egg, 1 teaspoon cinnamon and milk in a large bowl or mixer and beat until light and fluffy. Spread the mixture into the tin. It won't look like a very thick layer, but don't panic – all will be well. Carefully arrange the apple slices on top of the sponge mixture so they cover the sponge completely in an even layer. Sprinkle the crumble mixture over the top and bake for about 1 hour – a skewer will easily slip past the cooked apples and come out cleanly when the cake is done.

Mix together the remaining cinnamon and the demerara sugar and sprinkle over the top of the warm crumble. Leave in the tin until it is completely cold.

Banana cake

I make this easy cake in a loaf tin, but you don't have to – bung it in any cake tin you like and just tweak the timings. As with the carrot cake recipe on p.28, this is happy to have all manner of things added: walnuts, lemon or lime zest, dried cranberries and chocolate chips have all found their way into one of my banana cakes at some point. The other thing worth mentioning is that the riper the bananas, the better the cake, so don't chuck out soft blackish bananas – they are just the job.

✴ Serves 8

250 g/9 oz/1 cup plus 2 tbsp unsalted butter

225 g/8 oz/1 cup caster (superfine) sugar

2 large free-range eggs

3 large bananas, mashed

375 g/13 oz/3 ¾ cups self-raising flour, sifted

75 ml/2 ½ fl oz/scant ⅓ cup milk

Heat the oven to 160°C/325°F/Gas mark 3. Grease and line a 1 kg/2 ¼ lb loaf tin (pan). Cream together the butter and sugar until really pale and fluffy. Beat in the eggs – don't worry about the curdling as this always happens.

Add the mashed bananas and then fold in the flour. Add the milk (and any flavouring or additions you have chosen) and carefully mix in without bashing all the air out. Tip the mixture into the tin and bake for about 50 minutes – a skewer will come out clean when the cake is cooked. Cool the cake in the tin.

Madeira cake

There are times when a classic cake is called for. Nothing too extreme or unexpected. A gentle cake. A Madeira is a gentle cake, I like to think. I can imagine little old ladies having a slice with a cup of tea, but when your back is turned, slipping a small medicine bottle of sherry out from under their cushion, having a quick swig and then tucking it away again. And then, when you catch them spluttering, they gently tap at their chest and wave a lacy hanky at you, blaming the cake. 'Crumbs! Crumbs!' they cry.

✳ Serves 12

175 g/6 oz/¾ cup unsalted butter

175 g/6 oz/¾ cup caster (superfine) sugar

3 large free-range eggs, beaten

150 g/5 oz/1 ⅓ cups self-raising flour

100 g/3 ½ oz/scant 1 cup plain (all-purpose) flour

2 tbsp milk

1 tsp vanilla extract

Preheat the oven to 160°C/325°F/Gas mark 3. Grease and line a 1 kg/2 lb loaf tin (pan). In a mixer, or with an electric whisk, beat together the butter and sugar until really pale and fluffy. Very slowly beat in the eggs, a little at a time. Sift both flours over the egg mixture and very gently fold them in, followed by the milk and vanilla extract. Spoon the mixture into the tin and level the top. Bake for about 1 hour, or until firm to the touch.

This is a cake that welcomes orange or lemon zest, chocolate chips, caraway seeds or cherries as decoration.

Battenburg

I adored Battenburg cake when I was a child. The colours, the ability to peel off the marzipan coat and dissect the cake into its individual parts – everything about it appealed to me. I hadn't eaten one for years (apart from a brief foray into the miniature world of the cupcake Battenburg), and so this book was just the excuse I needed. If you hate marzipan you can always wrap the whole shebang in sugar paste (rolled fondant), dyed or undyed – I'm not getting involved. This recipe makes two Battenburgs – one for you and one for your kitsch friend (or the freezer).

✳ Serves 8

175 g/6 oz/1 ½ cups self-raising flour, sifted

175 g/6 oz/¾ cup caster (superfine) sugar

175 g/6 oz/¾ cup soft margarine

3 large free-range eggs

1 tsp vanilla extract

pink food colouring

apricot jam (at least half a jar)

500 g/1 lb 2 oz marzipan

Preheat the oven to 160°C/325°F/Gas mark 3. Grease and line two 20 cm/8 in square sandwich tins (pans).

In a mixer, beat the flour, sugar, margarine, egg and vanilla until really pale and fluffy. Divide the mixture into two and carefully tint one half of the mixture pink. Leave the other half au naturel. Spread the mixture into the two tins, one colour in each, and bake for 15–20 minutes or until the cakes are firm and springy to the touch. Leave them to cool on wire racks.

Now the exciting bit. Sieve the apricot jam to get all the lumpy bits out, spread a thin layer of jam on the top of one of the cakes and then place the other cake on top. Trim the cakes so that they have really sharp, straight edges and then cut the double-layered cake into four equal strips. Take one strip and brush some jam along the long cut edge. Tip it on its side so that the jammy cut edge is facing upwards. Take another strip, invert it and lay it on top of the jammy edge so that a pink square lies next to a pale square. You should now have a naked-looking battenburg. Repeat this process with the other two strips.

Roll out the marzipan so that you have two rectangles of about 18 x 28 cm/7 x 11 in. Brush the whole of the outside edges of the cakes with jam and then place them on top of the marzipan and wrap it around the cakes. I then like to trim both ends to give a lovely sharp end. Wrap both cakes tightly in cling film (plastic wrap), retaining their square shape, and leave for a couple of hours for the marzipan and the sponge to get acquainted.

Red velvet cake

Oh, how I battled with this. Should it be in the Posh section, or should it be Everyday? Do you know what? I am still undecided. It is a super scrumptious cake. It's not tricky, but not the simplest either. I do, however, implore you with all my heart to try it. A red velvet cake is one that demands to be baked, and I suppose it is those demands that made me put it into this chapter.

✱ Serves 10

60 g/2 oz/¼ cup unsalted butter or soft margarine

150 g/5 oz/⅔ cup caster (superfine) sugar

1 large free-range egg, beaten

30 g/1 oz/¼ cup cocoa powder

1 tsp vanilla extract

red food colouring

125 ml/4 fl oz/½ cup buttermilk

150 g/5 oz/1 ⅓ cups plain (all-purpose) flour, sifted

1 ½ tsp red wine vinegar

½ tsp bicarbonate of soda (baking soda)

150 g/5 oz/⅔ cup unsalted butter

600 g/1 lb 5 oz/4 ½ cups icing (confectioners') sugar, sifted

1 tsp vanilla extract

200 g/7 oz/generous ¾ cup cream cheese

Preheat the oven to 160°C/325°F/Gas mark 3. Grease and line three 20 cm/8 in sandwich tins (pans). Beat the butter or soft margarine and caster (superfine) sugar in a mixer (or with an electric hand whisk) until really pale and fluffy. Slowly add the egg, beating wildly as you go.

In a separate bowl, mix together the cocoa, vanilla extract and some red food colouring until you have a thick, dark paste. Then add 1 teaspoon of water at a time and mix well until the mixture just starts to run a bit (but it should still be pretty thick). Add this to the buttery egg mixture and beat well until it is all incorporated. Add half the buttermilk and give it a good beat, then add half the flour and beat again. Repeat this process with the remaining buttermilk and flour. Finally add the vinegar and the bicarbonate of soda (baking soda) and beat away for another 1–2 minutes.

Divide the mixture between the three tins and bake for about 25 minutes or until a skewer comes away cleanly. Cool the cakes on a wire rack.

To make the frosting (I say 'frosting' because this is an American cake and I am using the correct lingo), beat together the butter, icing (confectioners') sugar, vanilla and cream cheese until fluffy and spreadable. You may need to add a bit more sugar if it is all too runny, or maybe a drop or two of milk if it is too thick. Do taste as you go, though, and make sure you've got enough vanilla in there.

Sandwich the cakes together with a thin layer of frosting and then spread the remains over the top and sides of the cake. Golly, it's good.

Man cake

Perhaps I should explain. I made this sultana cake intending it to be just that – a sultana cake. My husband and his man chums completely appropriated it, cut it into man-chunks (it was originally round), stuffed it into their rucksacks and went off playing on their mountain bikes. They came back all muddy and cheerful and said that the cake was a great success. I gave them a withering look and told them to take their shoes off.

✳ Serves 8–10

450 g/1 lb/4 ½ cups plain (all-purpose) flour

2 tsp mixed spice

1 tsp cinnamon

1 tsp bicarbonate of soda (baking soda)

175 g/6 oz/¾ cup unsalted butter

225 g/8 oz/1 ¼ cups light brown soft sugar

225 g/8 oz/1 ½ cups sultanas (golden raisins)

1 large free-range egg, beaten

300 ml/½ pt/1 ¼ cups milk

150 g/5 oz/¾ cup sugarcubes

Preheat the oven to 160°C/325°F/Gas mark 3. Grease and line a deep 20 cm/8 in loose-bottomed cake tin (pan).

Sift the flour, spices and bicarbonate of soda (baking soda) into a large bowl and rub in the butter, aiming for a texture like fine breadcrumbs. Stir in the sugar and the sultanas (golden raisins). Mix in the egg and milk and stir away until you have a soft dropping consistency – in other words, it plops gently off the spoon without having to waggle it. You may need to add a little more milk if it doesn't plop nicely.

Transfer the mixture to the tin and even out the top. Bash the sugarcubes up a bit (I do it in a pestle and mortar) so that you have uneven gravel rather than sand, and scatter it over the top of the cake.

Bake for about 1 hour 20 minutes or until a knife or skewer comes out clean – check after about an hour. Cool in the tin for about 10 minutes before finishing off the cooling process on a wire rack. Watch a man come along and hack it to pieces and wander off muttering about spokes.

Cherry and coconut cake

This is a shamelessly retro cake. There is something deeply unfashionable about glacé (candied) cherries and desiccated coconut, so of course I feel I must use them. I am proud of my love for this cake. People may want to eat it hiding in a corner, but I bet they really enjoy it. Fly the flag for cherry and coconut, I say. Hurrah to you both.

✴ Serves 8–10

125 g/4 ½ oz/½ cup plus
   1 tbsp unsalted butter

250 g/9 oz/2 ¼ cups self-raising
   flour, sifted

100 g/3 ½ oz/1 ⅓ cups
   desiccated coconut

125 g/4 ½ oz/scant 1 cup caster
   (superfine) sugar

225 ml/7 ½ fl oz/scant
   1 cup milk

2 large free-range eggs

125 g/4 ½ oz/¾ cup glacé
   (candied) cherries, rinsed,
   dried and finely chopped

Preheat the oven to 160°C/325°F/Gas mark 3. Grease and line a 1 kg/2 lb loaf tin (pan). Rub the butter into the flour until you have a breadcrumb consistency and then stir in the sugar, 75 g/2 ½ oz/1 cup coconut and the sugar. In a jug, whisk together the milk and eggs and then pour onto the dry mixture and give it a good old beating.

Pop the mixture into the tin and scatter the remaining coconut on top of the cake. Bake for about 1 hour, checking it at around the 40–45 minute stage. The cake won't be cooked, but you will probably need to cover it with greaseproof paper (parchment paper) to stop the top from over-browning (technical term for burning).

Turn out the cake onto a wire rack to cool and present it to your coolest, hippest friends.

Apple and ginger cake

This recipe was given to me by my friend Claire, and I am truly grateful, because it is such a cracker of a cake. The fresh ginger is warming; the apple means that it keeps incredibly well; the crunchy top adds another texture – it is now one of my all-time favourite cakes. I gave a great wodge of it to Doreen, my favourite 85-year-old cake tester. Her comment: 'It's lovely as a cake, but really comes alive with a bit of custard and cream.' Now there's a woman who understands cake.

✳ Serves 8

110 g/4 oz/½ cup unsalted butter

225 g/8 oz/1 ¼ cups dark muscovado sugar

2 large free-range eggs, beaten

60 g/2 oz/¼ cup fresh root ginger, peeled and grated

225 g/8 oz/2 cups self-raising flour

280 g/10 oz/1 ½ cups peeled and diced apples

2 tbsp runny honey

2 tbsp demerara sugar

Preheat the oven to 160°C/325°F/Gas mark 3 and grease and line a deep 20 cm/8 in cake tin (pan). Cream together the butter and muscovado sugar until pale and fluffy. Slowly add the eggs, bit by bit, beating well between each addition. Tip in the ginger and mix it all in. Then sift the flour over the top and fold it in, followed by the apple.

Tip the mixture into the tin and even it all out. Bake for about 50–60 minutes – it's done when it's firm and springy and a skewer or knife inserted comes out clean.

Mix the honey and the demerara sugar together and spread it all over the cake as soon as it comes out of the oven. Leave to cool in the tin – although I do believe that Doreen would scoop it straight out of the tin and pop it in a bowl with a good glug of custard, given half a chance.

Famous five cake

'Well, Ann,' said Julian, his hands on his hips, 'what have you got for us to eat? I'm simply ravenous!' Ann looked into her wicker basket, covered with a jolly tea towel. 'Oh Julian, you and Dick just had the most enormous breakfast. How can you possibly be hungry?' 'Oh, you silly old baby, Ann,' said Julian, 'you wouldn't understand. Just give me some cake and go and do some washing up.' Ann picked up a slab of the most scrumptious fruit cake which was nestling under a bag of tomatoes and whacked her brother round the ear. 'Take that, you beastly boy,' shrieked Ann. 'That's the last bit of baking I ever do for you.' 'Respect,' said George.

✳ Serves 8–10

225 g/8 oz/1 cup unsalted butter

225 g/8 oz/1 cup caster (superfine) sugar

4 large free-range eggs, beaten

275 g/9 ½ oz/2 ⅔ cups self-raising flour, sifted

½ tsp cinnamon

½ tsp ground ginger

½ tsp mixed spice

50 g/1 ¾ oz/⅓ cup raisins

25 g/1 oz/2 ½ tbsp ready-to-eat dried apricots, chopped

25 g/1 oz/2 ½ tbsp stoned and chopped dates

2 tbsp milk

2 tbsp demerara sugar

Preheat the oven to 160°C/325°F/Gas mark 3. Grease and line an 18 cm/7 in square tin (pan). Cream the butter and sugar until really pale and then add the eggs, a little at a time. Fold in the sifted flour, the spices and the dried fruit, add the milk and give it a careful stir. The mixture needs to gently plop off the spoon. If it doesn't, add a little more milk.

Tip the mixture into the tin and level it out. Sprinkle the demerara sugar over the cake and bake for about 45 minutes, or until springy to the touch and a skewer or knife comes out clean. Leave to cool in the tin.

HRH fave cake

I inherited my grandmother's recipe book, chock full of scraps of paper, bits of envelope and the backs of intriguing half-letters, all covered with her familiar scrawl. This piece of paper caught my eye: grey Basildon Bond and typed on an old typewriter. There's no sign of who it came from, but it's very seriously headed 'Queen Elizabeth the Queen Mother's Favourite Cake'. Flipping heck! I can imagine Granny taking that incredibly seriously. Tellingly, she never made it for us, though – not worthy. Essentially it is a lovely sticky toffee cake – probably very good in front of the races.

✳ Serves 8

150 g/5 oz/¾ cup stoned and chopped dates

1 tsp bicarbonate of soda (baking soda)

250 ml/8 fl oz/1 cup boiling water

200 g/7 oz/scant 1 cup caster (superfine) sugar

200 g/7 oz/scant 1 cup unsalted butter

250 g/9 oz/2 ¼ cups self-raising flour

1 large free-range egg, beaten

300 g/10 oz/1 ½ cups light muscovado sugar

4 tbsp double (whipping) cream

Preheat the oven to 160°C/325°F/Gas mark 3. Grease and line a 20 cm/8 in square cake tin (pan). Put the dates and the bicarbonate of soda (baking soda) in a bowl, pour the boiling water over and leave to soak for 5 minutes or so.

In a big bowl (or mixer), beat the caster (superfine) sugar, 50 g/1 ¾ oz/scant ¼ cup butter, flour and egg and then stir in the date-water-bicarb mix.

Put the mixture in the tin, level out the surface and bake for about 35 minutes or until firm and springy to the touch. Cool on a wire rack while you get on with the topping.

Put the muscovado sugar, remaining butter and the cream in a pan. Gently heat and then boil rapidly for 1–2 minutes. Leave the mixture to cool a little, then spread all over the cake and leave alone for 1–2 hours for the topping to fully set.

Butterscotch and walnut cake

This is a classic 'doesn't look much, but take it away before I wolf the whole thing' cake. Easy and utterly, utterly delicious.

✳ Serves 12

125 g/4 ½ oz/½ cup plus 1 tbsp unsalted butter

400 g/6 oz/2 cups light muscovado sugar

2 large free-range eggs, separated

1 tbsp golden syrup

150 ml/5 fl oz/⅔ cup milk

1 tsp vanilla extract

225 g/8 oz/2 cups self-raising flour

50 g/1 ¾ oz/scant ½ cup walnuts, chopped

2 tbsp milk

25 g/1 oz/1 ¾ tbsp unsalted butter

Preheat the oven to 160°C/325°F/Gas mark 3. Grease and line a 23 cm/9 in square tin (pan).

Cream together 100 g/3 ½ oz/scant ½ cup butter and 175 g/6 oz/¾ cup sugar until pale and fluffy. Beat in the egg yolks and then the syrup, 120 ml/4 fl oz/½ cup milk and the vanilla. If you're using a mixer, you really need to scrape down the sides of the bowl every now and again and do a bit more beating. Then sift the flour over the mixture and fold it in at the same time as the chopped walnuts. Whisk the egg whites until stiff and then fold these into the mixture too.

Pop the mixture into the tin and level the top. Bake for about 45 minutes, or until firm and springy to the touch. Cool the cake in the tin.

Put the remaining sugar, milk and butter in a pan and heat gently. Boil for about 5 minutes, then pour over the top of the cake and leave to soak in and set a little (it will always be deliciously sticky) before taking the whole thing into a quiet corner. If you can remember to take a mug of tea with you, all the better.

Chocolate orange loaf

This came about after pitiful pleadings from the husband. I'm not a huge fan of chocolate orange, but it would appear that plenty of other people are. The chief testers of this cake were all chocolate-orange aficionados and all stated that it passed muster. If you can get hold of proper orange extract (not flavouring), do use it, otherwise use real zest.

✳ Serves 8

150 g/5 oz/1 ¾ cups self-raising flour, sifted

30 g/1 oz/¼ cup cocoa powder

175 g/6 oz/¾ cup caster (superfine) sugar

175 g/6 oz/¾ cup soft margarine

3 large free-range eggs

grated zest of 2 large oranges or ½ tsp orange extract

110 g/4 oz/⅔ cup chocolate chips

Preheat the oven to 160°C/325°F/Gas mark 3. Grease and line a 1 kg/2 lb loaf tin (pan).

Place all the ingredients apart from the chocolate chips into a mixer and beat until the mixture is pale and mousse-like. Then carefully fold in the chocolate chips. If you don't get a lovely waft of orange at this stage, add more zest or more orange extract.

Tip the mixture into the loaf tin and level the surface. Bake for about 1 hour 15 minutes – you may need to cover the top of the cake after about 50 minutes. Test the cake by inserting a knife or skewer – it will come out clean when it is done. Cool on a wire rack.

Carrot and courgette cake

Now don't be going all sniffy and screwing up your face. Would I bother with a recipe that was disgusting? No, I wouldn't. Carrots and courgettes both work in exactly the same way in a cake – they add moistness and texture without turning it into some sort of savoury weirdness. Cardamom is a fantastic spice which is much underused, I think. It gives the cake a wonderful Middle Eastern feel, but you can leave it out if this makes you happier.

✳ Serves 8

1 tsp cardamom pods

125 g/4 ½ oz/scant ⅔ cup caster (superfine) sugar

125 ml/4 fl oz/½ cup sunflower oil

3 large free-range eggs, beaten

125 g/4 ½ oz/1 ¼ cups self-raising flour

1 tsp bicarbonate of soda (baking soda)

1 tsp ground cinnamon

25 g/1 oz/⅓ cup desiccated coconut

75 g/2 ½ oz/½ cup pistachios, chopped

110 g/4 oz/⅔ cup carrot, peeled and grated

75 g/2 ½ oz/½ cup courgette, grated

Preheat the oven to 160°C/325°F/Gas mark 3. Grease and line a 1 kg/2 lb loaf tin (pan). Prepare the cardamom by splitting the little pods open and scraping out the black seeds into a pestle and mortar. Discard the husks and pound the black seeds to a powder.

In a large bowl, whisk together the sugar and the oil really well. Then add the eggs and give it another really good whisking. Sift the flour, bicarbonate of soda (baking soda) and cinnamon over the mixture. Add the coconut, cardamom and the pistachios and fold in carefully. Then add the grated vegetables and fold them in, too. Pour the mixture into the tin and bake for about 50 minutes or until firm to the touch and a knife or skewer comes out clean. Leave to cool in the tin.

Citrus sensation

I love, love, love this cake! Of course, I adore the food colouring which gives it a proper 1970s vibe. You may, however, choose to leave off the colour. You don't have to use apricot jam, either – orange or lemon curd would also be gorgeous.

✳ Serves 8–10

225 g/8 oz/2 cups self-raising flour, sifted

225 g/8 oz/1 cup caster (superfine) sugar

225 g/8 oz/1 cup soft margarine

4 large free-range eggs

zest and juice of 2 oranges

orange food colouring

zest and juice of 1 lemon

yellow food colouring

2 tbsp apricot jam

3 tbsp icing (confectioners') sugar, sifted

Preheat the oven to 160°C/325°F/Gas mark 3. Grease and line three 20 cm/8 in sandwich tins (pans). In a mixer, beat together the flour, caster (superfine) sugar, margarine and eggs. When the mixture is pale and fluffy, divide the mixture between two bowls – two thirds in one bowl and the remaining third in another. Fold the orange zest and orange colouring into the larger quantity and divide between two of the three tins. Fold the lemon zest and the yellow colouring into the remaining bowl and pop that into the third tin. Bake the cakes for about 20 minutes, or until all are springy to the touch. Cool them all on wire racks.

When the cakes are cold, sandwich them together (orange cake, followed by lemon cake, followed by orange cake) with the jam.

Make a thin icing with the icing (confectioners') sugar and the orange and lemon juice – you won't need all the juice, so just add a little at a time. You want to have a consistency like double (whipping) cream. Pour over the top of the cake and let it dribble down the sides. Leave the cake for 1–2 hours for the icing to set. Weirdly (for me), I don't think the icing needs any extra colour adding.

Chocolate-Malteser-Nutella cake

This came about after one of those moments at eight o'clock in the evening when you realize that you were meant to take a cake to school the next day for some vital event. I launched myself into the kitchen and started rummaging. This is the end result and, to be honest, perhaps I should do more manic evening baking forays – it's a really yummy and easy cake. The massive plus point is that you can get loads of pieces out of it.

✳ Serves 24

200 g/7 oz/scant 2 cups self-raising flour

25 g/1 oz/¼ cup cocoa powder

225 g/8 oz/1 cup caster (superfine) sugar

225 g/8 oz/1 cup soft margarine

4 large free-range eggs

1 x 135 g/4 oz bag Maltesers

4 tbsp Nutella (or any other chocolate spread)

25 g/1 oz/1 ¾ tbsp unsalted butter

200 g/7 oz milk chocolate

100 ml/3 ½ fl oz/scant ½ cup double (whipping) cream

decorative sugar sprinkles (optional)

Preheat the oven to 160°C/325°F/Gas mark 3. Grease and line two 28 x 40 cm/11 x 16 in sandwich tins (pans).

Sift the cocoa and flour into a bowl (or mixer, preferably). Add the sugar. Add the margarine and eggs and beat for 2 minutes until pale and fluffy. Divide the mixture between the two tins – it will look quite thin, but don't worry. Bake for 15–20 minutes or until the cakes are springy to the touch. Cool the cakes on wire racks.

Empty the Maltesers into a heavy, deep bowl or a plastic bag and bash them about a bit with a rolling pin or the base of a saucepan. You want sturdy rubble rather than fine gravel. When the cakes are cool, spread the Nutella over one of them and scatter the Maltesers over. Place the other cake on top and press down fairly firmly to squish the Maltesers into the Nutella.

Place a bowl over a pan of barely simmering water (not letting the base of the pan touch the water), put the butter, chocolate and cream in it and let them melt and ooze together. When the chocolate has melted, give the mixture a good old whisk around and pour over the top of the cake. Scatter with sprinkles if you wish. Leave for 1–2 hours before cutting into pieces.

Devon cider and apple cake

I live in Devon and so it was inevitable that there had to be a Devon apple cake. Now, you may know about Dorset apple cake, Somerset apple cake, Gloucestershire apple cake, Yorkshire apple cake. I could go on, but we have to draw a line, so here it is: Devon apple cake with Devonian cider. The best. Obviously.

✳ Serves 8–10

1 large cooking apple, peeled and chopped

50 g/1 ¾ oz/⅓ cup sultanas (golden raisins)

150 ml/5 fl oz/⅔ cup dry cider

115 g/4 oz/½ cup unsalted butter

115 g/4 oz/⅔ cup light soft brown sugar

2 large free-range eggs, beaten

225 g/8 oz/2 cups plain (all-purpose) flour

1 tsp baking powder

1 tsp allspice

1 tsp cinnamon

zest of 1 lemon, grated

1 tbsp demerara sugar

Preheat the oven to 180°C/350°F/Gas mark 4. Grease and line a 20 cm/8 in square tin (pan). Put the chopped apples and the sultanas in a bowl and cover them with the cider.

In another bowl, cream together the butter and the brown sugar until pale and fluffy, then gradually beat in the eggs. Sift the flour over the mixture and fold it in with the baking powder, spices and lemon zest. Finally, fold in the soaked fruit and the cider.

Spread the mixture into the prepared tin and sprinkle the demerara sugar on top. Bake for about 45 minutes or until the cake is springy to the touch and a skewer comes out clean. Cool on a wire rack.

Granny's chocolate biscuit cake

This is another recipe garnered from my granny's recipe collection. It is written on the back of a piece of headed notepaper from the family firm. The writing is very neat and in ink – not my granny's. Whose, I wonder? It's a rather more complicated version of the traditional melt-chocolate-mix-with-broken-biscuits recipe, but very rich and scrumptious. The addition of brandy (which works very well) would elevate this no-cook cake into the 'posh' chapter.

✳ Serves 10–12

250 g/9 oz dark (bittersweet) chocolate (at least 70% cocoa solids)

225 g/8 oz/1 cup unsalted butter

2 large free-range eggs

2 tsp caster (superfine) sugar

225 g/8 oz digestive biscuits, broken into large gravel-size chunks

75 g/2 ½ oz/½ cup walnuts, chopped

75 g/2 ½ oz/¼ cup glacé (candied) cherries, chopped

2 tbsp brandy (optional)

Grease a loose-bottomed 20 cm/8 in cake tin (pan). Place a bowl over a pan of barely simmering water, being careful not to let the base of the bowl touch the water. Break up the chocolate and leave in the bowl to melt. Melt the butter in a separate pan and set aside.

In a large bowl, whisk the eggs with the caster (superfine) sugar until very pale and frothy. With the whisk still going, add the butter in a slow, steady stream. Add the melted chocolate and whisk that in, too.

Carefully stir in the broken biscuits, the walnuts and the cherries and mix it all up. Add the brandy if you are using it. Pop the mixture into the tin and smooth the surface. Leave in the fridge for about 4 hours (or overnight, preferably) to set.

To remove the cake from the tin, warm the outside of the tin with a hot cloth or carefully run it under the tap (without letting any water come into contact with the surface of the cake) and carefully push the base up and out of the main tin. You can then slide a palette knife under the base to free the cake.

Orange and sultana cake

Sultanas seem to be a bit of a mainstay of mine for everyday cakes. I think they are just fantastic in what are, essentially, fuel cakes. Dried fruit keeps you going and adds a natural sweetness to the proceedings. It goes well with citrusy flavours, so sultanas and oranges were always going to be a marriage made in heaven.

✳ Serves 12

275 g/9 ½ oz/1 ¾ cups sultanas (golden raisins)

grated zest and juice of 4 oranges

275 g/9 ½ oz/⅔ cup self-raising flour

225 g/8 oz/1 cup caster (superfine) sugar

225 g/8 oz/1 cup soft margarine

4 large free-range eggs

1 tsp baking powder

2 tbsp milk

3 tbsp demerara sugar

Soak the sultanas (golden raisins) in three-quarters of the orange juice for about 1 hour. Preheat the oven to 160°C/325°F/Gas mark 3 and grease and line a 28 x 40 cm/11 x 16 in sandwich tin (pan).

Sift the flour into the mixer bowl, add the sugar, margarine, eggs, baking powder and orange zest and beat until the mixture is pale and fluffy. Add the milk if the mixture is a bit thick (you may not need it all) until you get a soft dropping consistency. Fold in the sultanas (golden raisins) and spread the mixture into the prepared tin. Bake for about 30 minutes, or until the cake is firm and springy to the touch.

Mix the remaining orange juice with the demerara sugar and spread it over the cake while it's still warm – if you need a little more liquid, add more orange juice if you have any, or a teaspoon of runny honey. Leave the cake in its tin to cool and absorb the juice.

Lemony yogurt cake

In the olden days, when we were young and carefree, we used to go skiing. By tea time we were all ravenous and would pile back to the chalet, where a wonderful person would have rustled up a cake. Invariably it would be a yogurt cake, which was about the only cake that would rise at that altitude (apparently). Anyway, leaving the science behind, they were always delicious and so I present my version of the skiing-yogurt cake.

✳ Serves 8

200 g/7 oz/scant 1 cup unsalted butter

140 g/4 ¾ oz/scant ⅔ cup caster (superfine) sugar

3 large free-range eggs

zest and juice of 2 large unwaxed lemons

250 g/9 oz/2 ¼ cups plain (all-purpose) flour

1 tsp baking powder

150 g/5 oz/⅔ cup Greek yogurt

Preheat the oven to 160°C/325°F/Gas mark 3. Grease and line a 1 kg/2 lb loaf tin (pan). Beat together the butter and sugar until really pale and fluffy then beat in the eggs, one at a time. Then add the lemon zest and beat away for a couple of minutes. Sift the flour and the baking powder over the mixture and carefully fold it in. Finally add the lemon juice and the yogurt, folding well and making sure that everything is amalgamated.

Pop the mixture into the tin and level the surface. Bake for about 50 minutes, or until a skewer comes out cleanly. Leave the cake to cool in the tin for 10 minutes or so and then finish cooling on a wire rack.

Posh cakes

Now then, by 'posh' I mean not only showing-off cakes, but also cakes that require an amount of faffing. Some of the posh jobs don't actually need much faffing, but there's something about them that makes a journey into the everyday tin seem entirely inappropriate (courgette and elderflower, apricot and cardamom ...). However, if you're extremely grand, you may choose to have cakes like this in your everyday tin – far be it from me to dictate what you eat and when.

A cake like the Gâteau St. Honoré is a veritable fiesta of faffdom. I embrace cakes like this only occasionally, but it is so lovely to have a recipe in your armoury that you can whip out and use to truly impress that annoying person who thinks that they know everything about everything. I know one shouldn't use baked products as forms of one-upmanship. Very poor show, and all that, but sometimes, just sometimes, I find it hugely rewarding to present a piece of confectional perfection to just shut someone up. I'm not proud of this, but felt I should be honest about my character defects. Sorry.

Margarine doesn't show up much in this chapter, but unsalted butter, dark (bittersweet) chocolate, alcohol, cream and all sorts of premium ingredients are flung around. Buy the best ingredients you can – it's not rocket science: the better the ingredients, the better the end result.

Cakes for celebrations, such as weddings, grown-up birthdays, Christmas and Easter, all feature in this chapter, but as usual I have taken some rather grand liberties. Why on earth would I write a recipe for a Christmas cake that has been done a hundred times already – and very well? You want marzipan and royal icing? You've got it – but with sponge underneath. You can always adapt bonkers recipes like these to suit other occasions. There's no reason why this wouldn't make a perfectly good wedding cake. Aunt Edna might not approve – but you can get her round later for a slice of Gâteau St. Honoré.

Drunken prune and chocolate cake

Prunes and chocolate go really well, and you could actually state that a cake like this should be part of a regular diet (the emphasis on regular, if you know what I mean). However, purists might have a problem with the sugar, almonds, brandy, butter ... This is definitely a grown-up pudding cake and unless you have a fairly gung-ho attitude towards table manners, I'd insist on some form of cutlery to help get it from plate to mouth.

✳ Serves 12

150 g/5 oz/⅔ cup ready-to-eat dried prunes, whole

125 ml/4 fl oz/½ cup brandy

150 g/5 oz dark (bittersweet) chocolate (at least 70% cocoa solids)

225 g/8 oz/1 cup unsalted butter

225 g/8 oz/1 cup soft light brown sugar

4 large free-range eggs, separated

200 g/7 oz/2 ⅓ cups ground almonds

1 tsp baking powder

300 g/10 oz/1 ⅔ cups ready-to-eat dried prunes, roughly chopped

50 g/1 ¾ oz/scant ½ cup plain (all-purpose) flour

200 ml/7 fl oz/scant 1 cup double (whipping) cream

dark (bittersweet) chocolate for grating on top (optional)

First, soak the whole prunes in the brandy and set them aside to have a bit of a wallow. Preheat the oven to 160°C/325°F/Gas mark 3 and grease and line a loose-bottomed 20 cm/8 in cake tin (pan) – it needs to be quite deep, so not a sandwich tin.

In a bowl over a pan of barely simmering water, melt the chocolate and set it to one side. Then cream the butter and sugar together and beat in the egg yolks, one by one. Scrape down the bowl with a spatula and then beat in the melted chocolate, followed by the ground almonds.

In a separate, very clean bowl whisk the egg whites until they reach stiff peaks and then fold them into the chocolate and almond mixture. It is much easier if you do this in two or three goes.

Put the chopped prunes into a bowl, sprinkle them with the flour and toss them around a bit (sinkage prevention), then add them to the cake mixture and fold them in.

Put the mixture into the tin and bake for about 1 ½ hours. After about an hour, I tend to cover the top of the cake with greaseproof paper (parchment paper) to prevent it scorching. The cake is done when a skewer inserted comes out clean.

Leave the cake to cool in the tin. When it's cold, remove it from the tin, peel off the greaseproof paper and put the cake on a suitably grand plate. Lightly whip the cream so that it reaches soft peaks – don't over-whip it. Pile the cream on the top of the cake and then top with the plump, completely sozzled prunes that have been gently singing in their bath for the whole time. A grating of chocolate may be gilding the lily, but gild away, I say.

Chocolate torte

Sometimes there's a need for a simple, deeply chocolatey torte. No pastry. No frills. No decoration. A really intense hit of good-quality chocolate with just a bit of cream and maybe a few raspberries on the side reaches the spot. Ooh – maybe a glass of pudding wine is also called for. By the way, this torte is gluten-free, too.

✳ Serves 12

150 g/5 oz dark (bittersweet) chocolate (at least 70% cocoa solids)

150 g/5 oz/⅔ cup unsalted butter

100 g/3 ½ oz/scant 1 cup caster (superfine) sugar

4 large free-range eggs, separated

200 g/7 oz/2 ⅓ cups ground almonds

1 tbsp instant coffee granules made up to 3 tbsp with boiling water

Preheat the oven to 160°C/325°F/Gas mark 3. Grease and line a 20 cm/8 in cake tin (pan) – a removable base is a good idea. Put the chocolate, butter and sugar into a heatproof bowl and place it over a pan of barely simmering water, making sure the base of the bowl doesn't touch the water. Give the mixture a stir every now and then. When it's all dissolved and is smooth and glossy, tip it into a big mixing bowl and let it cool a little. One by one, beat in the egg yolks, followed by the ground almonds and the coffee.

In a separate, very clean bowl, whisk the egg whites until they're stiff. Quickly beat in one dessertspoon of the egg white to the chocolate mixture to loosen it up a bit, then fold in the egg whites in two goes. Turn the mixture into the tin and bake for about 1 hour or until a skewer comes out clean. Leave the cake to cool in the tin and serve either barely warm or at room temperature.

Hazelnut cake

There simply isn't a clever, snazzy title for this cake. It's a cake made from hazelnuts. It's light, it's simple and it really is rather posh.

✳ Serves 8

250 g/9 oz/1 ½ cups hazelnuts

4 large free-range eggs, separated

150 g/5 oz/⅔ cup caster (superfine) sugar

1 tsp baking powder

icing (confectioners') sugar, to dust

Preheat the oven to 160°C/325°F/Gas mark 3. Grease and line a 20 cm/8 in loose-bottomed cake tin (pan).

First, blanch the hazelnuts in boiling water for 30 seconds, drain them and pop them onto a clean tea towel. Place another tea towel over the top and rub like fury – the skins should come off easily. Then put the naked hazelnuts in a large dry frying pan and heat. Watch like a hawk and rattle the pan around so that they don't burn. When the nuts have taken on a golden hue, take them out and blitz them in a food processor until you get a fine powdery mass.

In a clean bowl, whisk together the egg yolks and sugar until really pale and fluffy. In a second clean bowl, whisk the egg whites until stiff. Fold the egg whites into the yolk and sugar mixture and finally fold in the hazelnuts and baking powder.

Put the mixture into the tin and bake for about 20–30 minutes until firm and springy to the touch. This type of nut-based cake can burn really easily, so keep an eye on the top of the cake and cover it with greaseproof paper (parchment paper) if you need to.

Leave the cake to cool in the tin. When it's completely cold, remove the cake from the tin and dust the top with icing (confectioners') sugar.

Summer sponge

The thing about a whisked sponge cake is that it needs eating the day it's made, so you have to make this simple cake as scrumptious as possible to ensure it gets scoffed. The way to guarantee no left-overs is to sandwich it together with such delicious summery things that no one can resist. So we're talking billowing cream, soft, succulent berries and, hey presto, it's gone.

✳ Serves 8

3 large free-range eggs, separated

75 g/2 ½ oz/⅓ cup caster (superfine) sugar

75 g/2 ½ oz/¼ cup plus 1 tbsp self-raising flour

150 ml/5 fl oz/⅔ cup double (whipping) cream

handful of very ripe soft fruit such as blackcurrants, strawberries, raspberries, or redcurrants

icing (confectioners') sugar, to dust

Preheat the oven to 160°C/325°F/Gas mark 3. Grease and line two 20 cm/8 in sandwich tins (pans).

Put the egg yolks and caster (superfine) sugar in a bowl and whisk until you have a very thick, pale and fluffy mixture. In another, very clean bowl, whisk the egg whites until they are stiff. Fold the egg whites into the egg yolk mixture. Then sift the flour over the mixture and, with a very light touch, fold the flour in. Divide the mixture between the two tins and bake for about 20 minutes or until firm to the touch. Turn the cakes out onto a wire rack to cool.

Whisk the cream until it's softly thick – don't overbeat it. When the cakes are cold, spread the cream over one of the cakes, scatter the fruit over the cream and top with the second cake.

Dust the top with a smattering of icing (confectioners') sugar and present your work to the crowds.

Pavlova

I'm not sure if this is a true Pavlova. The fruit can be changed to whatever you like – I can't think of a soft fruit that wouldn't work well.

✳ Serves 10

4 large free-range egg whites

225 g/8 oz/1 cup caster (superfine) sugar

300 ml/10 fl oz/1 ¼ cups double (whipping) cream

150 ml/5 fl oz/⅔ cup crème fraîche

500 g/1 lb 2 oz soft summery fruits such as raspberries, strawberries, or blackcurrants

Preheat the oven to its very lowest setting possible and line a large baking sheet with silicone paper. In a large, very clean bowl, whisk the egg whites until they reach firm peaks. Whisk in half the sugar until you have a smooth, shiny meringue, and then fold in the second half of the sugar.

Spoon the meringue onto the baking sheet and, with the back of a spoon, spread it out to your required shape (you decide if you want rectangular, square or round). It's also up to you how deep you want the meringue to be – you might prefer a deeper base with a marshmallow centre or a larger, thin, very crispy affair.

Place the meringue in the oven. Cooking times are completely arbitrary, I'm afraid. You are looking at a minimum of 2 hours, but it really depends how low your oven goes and how thick you have made your meringue. When the top of the meringue feels brittle to the touch and you can move the whole thing gently on its silicone paper, it's done.

You can make the meringue days in advance and keep it in an airtight container. Just before serving, whip the cream and pile it onto the meringue. Then top with the luscious fruits. Yummy.

Chocolate chestnut cake

Now, I must come clean here: I have never, ever made this cake with fresh chestnuts. Just too lazy. I like to pick up a nice packet of vacuum-packed chestnuts from the supermarket shelf that have been cooked and peeled for me. The topping comes from a can. Yes, a can. If it's good enough for the French, it's good enough for me.

✳ Serves 12

110 g/4 oz dark (bittersweet) chocolate (at least 70% cocoa solids)

450 g/1 lb cooked and peeled chestnuts

225 g/8 oz/1 cup caster (superfine) sugar

110 g/4 oz/½ cup unsalted butter, softened

5 large free-range eggs, separated

100 g/3 ½ oz/scant 1 ¼ cups ground almonds

240 g/9 oz can chestnut purée (marron glacé)

150 ml/5 fl oz/⅔ cup double (whipping) cream

dark (bittersweet) chocolate for decorating (optional)

Preheat the oven to 180°C/350°F/Gas mark 4. Grease and line a 20 cm/8 in loose-bottomed deep cake tin (pan). Melt the chocolate in a bowl set over a pan of barely simmering water, taking care the water doesn't touch the bowl, and set aside to cool slightly.

In a food processor or even a potato masher, mush up the chestnuts until you get a smoothish paste. In a large bowl (preferably attached to a mixer) beat together the sugar and butter until pale and creamy. Beat in the egg yolks, chestnut mush, melted chocolate and ground almonds.

In a separate bowl, whisk the egg whites until stiff and then fold them into the chocolate and chestnut mixture in two or three goes. Pour the mixture into the tin and bake for about 1 hour 10 minutes or until a knife or skewer comes out clean. Cool in the tin.

When the cake is cold, slip it out of its tin and place on a plate. Beat the chestnut pureé a bit to smooth it out and then spread it all over the cold cake. Whip the cream until it reaches soft peaks (don't whip it too firmly – it shouldn't be stiff), and then gently plop the cream onto the chestnut purée. If you like, grate some dark (bittersweet) chocolate over the top.

Strawberry shortcake

This is a bit of an English garden party classic, don't you think? The rules are simple: it must only be made in the summer when local strawberries are at their sweetest, juiciest best. Do me a favour – don't make it in the winter with tasteless, watery imported strawberries. Pointless. You can, of course, make this as little individual shortcakes or like this, as one big whopper.

✳ Serves 10

500 g/1 lb 2 oz/4 ¾ cups unsalted butter, softened

100 g/3 ½ oz/scant ½ cup caster (superfine) sugar

500 g/1 lb 2 oz/4 ¾ cups plain (all-purpose) flour

250 g/9 oz/1 ⅔ cups cornflour (cornstarch)

600 ml/1 pt/2 ½ cups double (whipping) cream

approx 1 kg/2 lb fresh strawberries, hulled and halved or quartered

icing (confectioners') sugar, to dust

Preheat the oven to 160°C/325°F/Gas mark 3. Grease and line three 20 cm/8 in sandwich tins (pans). In a large bowl, cream together the butter and sugar until pale and fluffy, and then sift the flour and cornflour (cornstarch) onto the butter mixture. Mix until you have a lovely smooth dough.

Divide the dough between the three tins and, with your fingers, press the dough into the tins, right up to the edges. Pop the tins into the fridge for about 30 minutes and then bake for 30–40 minutes until pale and golden. As soon as the shortcakes are out of the oven, get a knife and score portion lines onto the cakes (don't go all the way through). Leave the shortcakes to cool in their tins.

Lightly whip the cream so that it stands in peaks, but be careful not to overwhip it. To assemble the cake, place a little blob of cream onto the plate you are going to use – this stops the shortbread slipping around. Place the base shortbread onto the plate and gently spread half the cream over. Evenly scatter half the strawberries over the cream and gently place another shortbread on top, trying to line up the scored lines to make cutting easier. Then repeat the process, ending with naked shortbread as the top layer. A gentle sprinkling of icing (confectioners') sugar is all that is required – and a cup of Earl Grey.

Chocolate meringue tower

How lovely is this? Crisp chocolatey meringue with little bits of roasted hazelnut, giving it a note of nuttiness and oodles of rich, velvety chocolate custardy gorgeousness. It's the sort of affair that makes you want to lick the plate, which I do believe is frowned upon in smarter circles.

✳ Serves 12

50 g/1 ¾ oz/½ cup hazelnuts

6 large free-range eggs, separated (reserve 3 of the egg yolks in a separate bowl)

375 g/10 oz/1 ½ cups caster (superfine) sugar

50 g/1 ¾ oz/scant ½ cup cocoa powder

1 large free-range egg, plus 3 yolks (reserved from the quantity above)

350 ml/12 fl oz/1 ½ cups milk

150 ml/5 fl oz/⅔ cup double (whipping) cream

75 g/2 ½ oz/⅓ cup caster (superfine) sugar

45 g/1 ½ oz/¼ cup cornflour (cornstarch)

1 tsp vanilla extract

150 g/5 oz dark (bittersweet) chocolate (at least 70% cocoa solids), melted

Preheat the oven to as low as it will possibly go, and line three baking sheets with silicone paper. Roast the hazelnuts in a dry frying pan, shaking them about frequently to stop them burning. When they have darkened and smell gloriously nutty, roll them in a clean tea towel to remove their skins and then chop them finely.

Whisk the 6 egg whites until stiff and then whisk in 150 g/ 5 oz/⅔ cup caster (superfine) sugar until the meringue is shiny and smooth. Sift the cocoa over the meringue and fold it in with a further 150 g/5 oz/⅔ cup caster sugar and the chopped hazelnuts. Divide the mixture between the three baking sheets and smooth into circles of approximately 20 cm/8 in diameter – what's most important is that they are all the same size. Bake in the oven for about 2 hours, or until the meringue is crispy on top.

To make the custard, put the milk and the cream into a pan, bring it up to the boil and then turn the heat off. In a bowl, whisk together the remaining caster sugar with the whole egg and 3 egg yolks. Slowly whisk in the cornflour (cornstarch) and give it a really good whisk to get it completely lump-free.

Pour the hot milk and cream over the egg mixture, whisking all the time, then pour the mixture back into the pan and gently heat while whisking. Keep on whisking while the custard cooks and thickens – this usually takes about 5 minutes. Taste the custard and make sure that there is no trace of a floury taste. If there is, just cook it for a little longer until the flouriness has gone.

Take the pan off the heat and whisk in the vanilla extract and the melted chocolate. Try not to spoon the entire pan into your mouth, but transfer it to a bowl and cover the surface of the custard with a disc of greaseproof paper (parchment paper) which will prevent a skin forming. Leave the custard to become thoroughly cold.

Sandwich the meringue discs with the cold custard and scatter with more hazelnuts if you wish.

James's fruit cake

I am particularly fussy about rich fruit cakes. I mean, really fussy. When my chum James gave me a piece of his fruit cake, I was blown away. It really is the best fruit cake I have ever tasted. I still can't quite believe he gave me the recipe and, yet more, agreed to let me put it in this book. All I ask is that, when you make this cake, send James a small 'thank you' vibe as you stir. Now then, practicalities: this mixture will make two 15 cm/6 in cakes or one whopper (for a wedding cake, for instance). James has also given it to me in loaf form. Essentially, like a lot of fruit cakes, it doesn't rise much so you really can play about with sizes and shapes of tin (pan) very easily and jiggle the cooking times to suit the size of cake.

* Makes two 15 cm/6 in cakes
800 g/1 ¾ lb mix of raisins, currants and sultanas (golden raisins)

100 g/3 ½ oz/¼ cup chopped mixed peel

100 g/3 ½ oz/¼ cup glacé (candied) cherries, halved

50 g/1 ¾ oz/2 tbsp glacé (candied) cherries, whole

150 ml/5 fl oz/⅔ cup alcohol (mixture of brandy, port and rum)

200 g/7 oz/scant 1 cup unsalted butter

200 g/7 oz/1 cup dark muscovado sugar

2 tbsp black treacle

1 tbsp golden syrup

1 tbsp thick-cut marmalade

1 tsp vanilla extract

225 g/8 oz/2 cups plain (all-purpose) flour

2 tsp mixed spice

1 tsp ground cloves

2 tsp ground cinnamon

pinch of salt

4 large free-range eggs

100 g/3 ½ oz/½ cup almonds, roughly chopped

50 g/1 ¾ oz/½ cup pecans, roughly chopped

25 g/1 oz/2 tbsp hazelnuts, roughly chopped

The day before the big bake, soak the fruit in the alcohol and leave to wallow. The next day, preheat the oven to 150°C/300°F/Gas mark 2. Grease and line the tins (pans) that you will be using.

Cream the butter and sugar together until really light and fluffy and then add the treacle, syrup, marmalade and vanilla and give it a good old beat. Sift the flour, spices and salt onto the creamy mixture and stir it all in well. Then add the eggs one at a time and mix well between each addition. Add the fruits and all the remaining alcohol that might be lurking and really mix everything in well. Add the nuts and mix them in.

Split the mixture between the tins or put it into the one whopper. Level the surface, and then, with the back of a spoon, make a shallow dent in the centre of the cake. Bake for about 3 hours, but this will depend on what sort of tin you are using. Test it by inserting a skewer. If it comes out cleanly, it is done. If not, put it back for 10–15 minutes and test again. You might need to repeat this process a few times. If the top is overbrowning, cover it with greaseproof paper (parchment paper) while you continue the baking.

When the beauty is done, let it cool in the tin for 20 minutes before turning it onto a wire rack. Then skewer the cake another 6–7 times and carefully pour about 3 tablespoons of your chosen liquor (or mix of liquors) over the top of it. Quickly bung it in a plastic bag and then in an airtight tin. You can continue feeding the cake every fortnight, but don't overdo it, or the cake will end up too wet. James says don't do it more than twice. What he says goes.

This is the sort of cake that keeps for months in a tin, and positively enjoys the experience. However, making it a week before it's needed won't result in anyone complaining about lack of flavour, believe me.

Rather classy Christmas cake

I say 'rather classy' because, unusually for me, there's no glitter, no lurid green icing – in fact, a plethora of rather sophisticated loveliness. A boiled fruit cake base may not seem special enough for a Christmas cake, but believe me, it really is lovely – especially if you anoint it with a glug of alcohol. An alternative is to use James's Fruit Cake (p.76), which then makes a luxurious, very rich cake that certainly serves 16–20 people.

✳ Serves 12–14

1 boiled fruit cake (p.27) or ½ quantity James's Fruit Cake (p.76) (simply halve the recipe ingredients)

brandy, rum or other spirit of your choice

4 tbsp apricot jam, sieved

approx 400 g/14 oz/2 ⅓ cups glacé (candied) fruit

whole nuts such as blanched almonds, walnuts and pecans (optional)

At least a few weeks before the big event, make the cake, poke about a dozen holes in the cake with a skewer, wrap it in greaseproof paper (parchment paper) and pop it in a tin. Every day or two, return to the tin, peel back the paper and drizzle a few spoonfuls of brandy (or whatever you are using) over the cake, then wrap it up again and leave for another week. Keep doing this until you are ready to decorate the cake.

Take the cake out of the tin and brush the top with a thin layer of the apricot jam. Arrange the glacé (candied) fruit artistically over the top, making sure that you can see no cake between the fruit. Do add nuts if you wish, but this is purely optional. When you are satisfied with your artwork, heat through the rest of the apricot jam and, when it is really runny, brush it carefully over the fruit, which not only helps it to set but gives it a lovely sheen to boot.

Christmas cupcakes

Right, let's get this over with: these little cakes aren't in the 'Little Cake' chapter because I thought it would be more confusing for you, dear reader. To me, it made sense for all the Christmas cakes to be together. Is that all right?

The only thing left to say is that these are a hoot, and those who hate Christmas cake seem to have no trouble snaffling them. Essentially, it's Christmas cake in a cupcake – but it's sponge, too. Something for everyone. These cakes keep really well because the marzipan and the royal icing seal everything.

✳ Makes 12

110 g/4 oz/1 cup self-raising flour, sifted

50 g/1 ¾ oz/scant ¼ cup caster (superfine) sugar

4 tsp mincemeat

110 g/4 oz/½ cup soft margarine

2 large free-range eggs

1 tsp ground cinnamon

300 g/10 oz/2 cups icing (confectioners') sugar, sifted

1 tbsp lemon juice

1 large free-range egg white

200 g/7 oz marzipan

2 tbsp apricot jam, sieved

food colouring

edible glitter (optional)

Preheat the oven to 160°C/325°F/Gas mark 3. Line a 12-hole muffin tin (pan) with muffin cases (cups). In a mixer or food processor, beat the flour, caster (superfine) sugar, mincemeat, margarine, eggs and cinnamon until the mixture is fluffy and mousse-like. Spoon the mixture into the muffin cases and bake for 15–20 minutes or until the cakes are springy and firm to the touch. Leave them to cool on a wire rack.

Make the royal icing by beating together the icing (confectioners') sugar, lemon juice and egg white. The mixture should stand up in stiff peaks and be very smooth and very white. If it isn't, you haven't beaten for long enough. If the texture is all wrong, adjust it by adding a little water if the mix is too stiff or more icing sugar if it is too wet.

Roll out the marzipan to about 3 mm/⅛ in thick and cut out circles to fit the tops of the cupcakes. Brush each cupcake with a little apricot jam and place the discs of marzipan on top. Tint the icing whatever colour you like and ice the top of the cakes. Leave to dry for a couple of hours.

Gather up the remaining marzipan and tint this with the food colouring, too. Make whatever Christmassy shapes you like – holly leaves and berries, stars, baubles and so on. Roll them in glitter if you wish. Using a tiny dab of icing, stick your marzipan shapes to the iced cakes. You can also put some of the icing into little piping (decorating) bags and pipe patterns over the top – let your imagination run riot. Leave for a good few hours to dry out properly before sharing your wares.

Rebel's Christmas cake

I love a bit of subversion. Not a lot, you understand, just a wink towards it every now and again. Most of my subversive tendencies present themselves in the form of cake. I don't know if this is something to worry about or be proud of. This cake is a case in point. To all intents and purposes, it looks like a pretty normal Christmas cake (granted, there are huge, edible glitter balls on top, but we won't worry about that). It's got royal icing, marzipan, but what is this? Lurking underneath, for those who hate Christmas cake – a sponge! This would be great with a chocolate cake, a red velvet or carrot – whatever you like. Don't leave out the marzipan, though – it gives a really smooth finish to ice on top.

✳ Serves 12

1 Victoria sponge (p.18) or a
  sponge cake of your choice

4 tbsp jam of your choice

1.5 kg/3 lb 3 oz marzipan

1 kg/2 lb icing (confectioners')
  sugar, sifted, plus extra for
  dusting

2 large free-range egg whites

juice of 2 large lemons

food colouring paste

edible glitter

Sandwich the two sponge cakes together with a large spoonful of jam. Sieve the rest of the jam into a small saucepan and set aside.

Roll out 1 kg/2 lb marzipan, using icing (confectioners') sugar to stop it sticking, until it is about 3 mm/⅛ in thick. Pop one of the cake tins (pans) onto the marzipan and cut round it. Then cut out a rectangle as long as your cake's circumference and as deep as its depth.

Warm the sieved jam until it's really loose, then carefully brush the whole of the top and sides of the cake. Put the circular top piece of marzipan on and carefully smooth it down to get rid of any air bubbles. Then wrap the strip of marzipan around the sides of the cake – the jam should act like a glue. When you are happy that all is smooth and wonderful, it's really best to leave the cake alone for a day. If you're in a tearing rush you can ice it now, but it's not as easy.

To make the icing, the easiest method is in a mixer. If you don't have one, use an electric hand whisk – you'd need arms like a shot putter to do this by hand. Place the icing sugar, egg whites and lemon juice in a very clean bowl and slowly start beating (I use the paddle beater rather than the whisk attachment). Turn up the speed slowly until you get to full turbo thrust. The icing should get whiter and whiter and more and more meringue-like. If your icing is a bit on the cement side, add a few drops of water. If it is too runny, add more icing sugar.

The consistency you are after is a white thick icing in which peaks stand up, but with one quick and gentle prod they keel over.

I find the easiest way to ice a cake like this is to put it on a cardboard cake board, which makes it sturdier straight away. Then place the cake on something like an upturned dish which is slightly smaller in circumference than the cake. This means you can get right to the very bottom of the cake without any difficulty.

So, you have your marzipanned cake in front of you – now to do some icing. A palette knife is invaluable here. Just plonk the icing on top first, and keep smoothing. Adding little and often to the sides is easier than trying to get a great dollop on, which just falls straight off. It doesn't have to be super-smooth, but if you're getting worked up about lack of smoothness, try dipping the palette knife into some hot water and smooth away your worries.

Leave the cake to dry while you crack on with the baubles. You should have about 500 g/1 lb 2 oz marzipan left. Give it a good old knead to make it flexible and then just pull off marble-sized balls and roll them up. I think it's good to have different-sized baubles, but it's up to you. Sprinkle some glitter onto a saucer, wet your hands and pick up a marzipan ball. Roll it around in your wet hand and then drop it onto the glitter and shake it around so that all the surfaces are covered. Keep going until you have as many glittery baubles as you want.

Place them onto the cake, using a tiny dab of royal icing as glue. Leave the cake for about 24 hours for the icing to dry out properly.

Simnel cake

I suppose this is the traditional Easter version of the ubiquitous Christmas cake. A lot of recipes seem to want to make yet another rather ordinary fruit cake. I make no apology for dragging out my favourite boiled fruit cake again. It really is fantastic to use as a base for this cake. Do alter the fruits if you like; sultanas, glacé (candied) cherries, currants – all good, but if the thought appals you, do use James's Fruit Cake (p.76)

✳ Serves 10

110 g/4 oz/¾ cup raisins

110 g/4 oz/¾ cup ready-to-eat dried apricots

50 g/1 ¾ oz/⅓ cup dried cherries

110 g/4 oz/1 ¼ cups dried peaches (or pears)

110 g/4 oz/½ cup unsalted butter

110 g/4 oz/⅔ cup light muscovado sugar

150 ml/5 fl oz/⅔ cup water

2 large free-range eggs, beaten

2 tsp mixed spice

225 g/8 oz/2 cups self-raising flour

1 kg/2 lb marzipan

1 tbsp apricot jam, sieved

1 large free-range egg, beaten (for brushing)

Preheat the oven to 150°C/300°F/Gas mark 2. Grease and line a 20 cm/8 in cake tin (pan). Put the fruit, butter, sugar and water into a saucepan and gently heat it until it comes up to simmering point. Simmer for about 20 minutes, stirring occasionally. When the mixture is cool, add 2 eggs and the spice and sift the flour over the top of it all. Chop up 200 g/7 oz marzipan into small chunks and add it to the mixture. Give it a good stir until everything is incorporated.

Tip the mixture into the tin and smooth the top. Bake for about 1 ½ hours, checking after 1 hour to see if it's done. Protect the top of the cake with some greaseproof paper (parchment paper) if it looks as if it's turning too dark.

Let the cake cool in the tin for about 20 minutes before turning out onto a wire rack. Roll out the rest of the marzipan until it is about 5 mm/¼ in thick and use the cake tin as a template to cut round. Spread the apricot jam over the top of the cake and place the marzipan disk on top. Then make your 'apostles', otherwise known as balls of marzipan. You can make either 11 or 12, depending on whether you want to include Judas or not.

Once you've reached your decision, brush the top of the cake with the beaten egg to make a sticky surface for your apostles to adhere to and give them a coat of it, too. Preheat the grill (broiler) to really hot and pop the cake under it. Do not walk away – do not even look away. When the marzipan has turned a glorious golden, toasty colour, whip the cake out sharpish.

Summer wedding cake

I've called this a wedding cake, but you could adapt it to any occasion. It's just a very pretty, summery affair and, for all its floral flourishes, really is a cinch to make. The Internet is a wonderful place, and online sugar craft shops sell absolutely everything you could ever want. As with many of the other special occasion cakes, do vary the sponge underneath if you like – I just love the citrusy tang of lemon in the summer.

✳ Serves approximately 60

For the main cake:

175 g/6 oz/1 ½ cups
    self-raising flour

175 g/6 oz/¾ cup caster
    (superfine) sugar

175 g/6 oz/¾ cup soft margarine

3 large free-range eggs

zest of 3 unwaxed lemons

For the cupcakes:

225 g/8 oz/2 cups
    self-raising flour

225 g/8 oz/1 cup caster
    (superfine) sugar

225 g/8 oz/1 cup soft margarine

4 large free-range eggs

zest of 4 unwaxed lemons

2 tbsp lemon curd

For the icing:

750 g/1 lb 10 oz/3 ¼ cups
    unsalted butter, softened

2 kg/4 ½ lb icing (confectioners')
    sugar, sifted

juice of 7 lemons

lemon oil (optional)

food colouring gel

For the decoration:

approx 60 wafer roses

50–60 sugar flowers such as
    pansies, daisies or roses

Start by making the main cake. Preheat the oven to 160°C/325°F/Gas mark 3 and grease and line one deep 16 cm/6½ in round cake tin (pan). Place all the ingredients for the cake except the lemon curd into a mixer and beat until really pale and fluffy. Tip the mixture into the tin and bake for about 45–60 minutes, or until a knife or skewer comes out cleanly. You may need to protect the top of the cake with some greaseproof paper (parchment paper) if it starts to over-brown. Cool the cake on a wire rack.

Then make the cupcakes in exactly the same way, except placing spoonfuls of the mixture into 48 cupcake cases (baking cups) which you have put into muffin trays. These will take 15–20 minutes to cook. Cool them on a wire rack.

To make the lemony icing, simply beat together the butter and the icing (confectioners') sugar until creamy, then add enough lemon juice to give you a smooth, spreadable texture and a good flavour. If you can get hold of some lemon extract, do add a few drops at this stage. Add the food colouring a tiny amount at a time, beating between each addition until you get the colour you are after.

Split the big cake into three, horizontally, and then sandwich the pieces back together with the lemon curd.

Spread some of the icing all over the top and the side of the cake and smooth it out; then, working quickly, start placing the wafer roses all over the cake, pushing them into the icing. Leave the cake alone for at least 6 hours to settle down after all the excitement.

Spread the rest of the icing over the cupcakes and decorate each cake with a single flower.

A grand affair

Cupcakes at a wedding? Outrageous, ghastly business! What one wants is a proper three-tiered cake that one can cut with the family sword – photographic opportunities for the family album. Cupcakes? Pah. Each tier is a different flavour here, which may upset traditionalists, but just don't tell them and give them a bit of the base fruit layer. They won't approve of the decoration, but then, they probably won't approve of the dress, the flowers, the groom, the bride, the cutlery...

✳ Serves around 200

For the base layer:

1 full quantity of James's Fruit Cake (p.76)

2.5 kg/5 ½ lb marzipan

1 jar apricot jam, sieved

3 kg/6 ½ lb white sugar paste (rolled fondant)

For the middle layer:

4 x quantities of Victoria Sponge (p.18)

1 jar apricot jam, sieved

1 jar strawberry jam, sieved

2 kg/4 ½ lb marzipan

2.5 kg/5 ½ lb white sugar paste (rolled fondant)

For the top layer:

1 ½ quantities of Basic Chocolate Cake (p.24)

2 tbsp Nutella

2 tbsp apricot jam, sieved

1 kg/2 lb marzipan

1.5 kg/3 lb 3 oz white sugar paste (rolled fondant)

For the decorations:

1 kg/2 lb white sugar paste (rolled fondant)

black food colouring gel

edible glue

½ quantity of royal icing (Rebel's Christmas Cake, p.82)

small quantity of vodka for brushing

First make the flowers by dyeing the sugar paste (rolled fondant) with black colouring gel – use rubber gloves for this! Roll out the paste (fondant), cut out about 200 flowers (you don't have to count them) and lay them on a sheet of silicone paper. Make a small indentation on the centre of each flower. Leave them to dry out thoroughly – you can do this at least a week in advance.

Make James's Fruit Cake as per the recipe on p.76 but use a 35 cm/14 in tin (pan). When baked, put it on a 35 cm/14 in cake board. Roll out the marzipan to about 3 mm/⅛ in thick. Spread the apricot jam over the cake and lay the marzipan over the top. Smooth it all out, getting rid of any air bubbles.

Bake the Victoria sponge in a 25 cm/10 in tin. When it is cooked and cooled, split it, spread the jam in the middle and put it on a cake board; repeat the marzipan process.

Bake the chocolate cake in a 17 cm/6 ¾ in tin, then split it, spreading Nutella in the middle, and put it on a cake board; again, repeat the marzipan process. Leave all three cakes with their marzipan coats for a day to dry out.

The next day, roll out all the sugar paste (rolled fondant) quantities to about 2 mm/⅛ in thick. Brush each marzipanned cake with a small amount of clear spirit such as vodka, and lay the paste (fondant) on top. Smooth the paste (fondant) over each cake and trim the bottoms.

Take half the royal icing, dye it black and put into a piping (decorating) bag with a fine nozzle (tube). Put the remaining white icing into another bag with a fine nozzle. Pipe a tiny dot into the centre of each of the flowers and leave to dry. With a small brush, gently stick each flower onto the cake with a tiny dab of edible glue. Choose whatever arrangement you like. Take the bag with the black icing and pipe tiny dots wherever suits.

To assemble the cake, place six plastic dowels in the bottom cake in a circular formation just within the diameter of the middle layer (25 cm/10 in). Place four dowels in the middle layer within the 17 cm/6 ¾ in diameter of the top layer. Carefully place the Victoria sponge on top of the fruit cake and the chocolate cake on top of this. Arrange some black ribbon around the base of each cake, securing it at the back with a pin. It is worth while having your piping bags handy at this stage, too, to make any last-minute piped adjustments once the cake is in situ.

Chocolate Easter cake

Now we're talking. Easter is one big chocolate fest, is it not? I do believe there is quite an important religious festival attached, but this is a book about cake and so we will discuss the merits of chocolate cake. A special one. With extra chocolate. Excellent.

✱ Serves 10

60 g/2 oz/¼ cup unsalted butter, softened

150 g/5 oz/⅔ cup caster (superfine) sugar

1 large free-range egg

25 g/1 oz/¼ cup cocoa powder, sifted

1 tsp vanilla extract

140 ml/4 ¾ oz/scant ⅔ cup buttermilk

150 g/5 oz/1 ⅓ cups plain (all-purpose) flour

½ tsp bicarbonate of soda (baking soda)

2 tsp red wine vinegar

For the icing:

125 g/4 ½ oz/½ cup plus 1 tbsp unsalted butter, softened

125 g/4 ½ oz/generous ½ cup cream cheese

500 g/1 lb 2 oz/about 3 ¼ cups icing (confectioners') sugar, sifted

100 g/3 ½ oz/¾ cup cocoa powder, sifted

80 ml/2 ½ fl oz/scant ⅓ cup milk

as many mini chocolate eggs as you can cram on top

Preheat the oven to 160°C/325°F/Gas mark 3. Grease and line a 20 cm/8 in loose-bottomed tin (pan). In a mixer, cream together the butter and caster (superfine) sugar until really pale and fluffy and then beat in the egg. Next, add the sifted cocoa and the vanilla extract and beat them in. Scrape down the bowl and beat in half the buttermilk followed by half the flour. Repeat this process and then add the bicarbonate of soda (baking soda) and vinegar and beat for a few more minutes. Scrape the mixture into the tin and bake for about 30–40 minutes or until a skewer comes out cleanly. Cool the cake on a wire rack.

To make the icing, beat together the butter and cream cheese and then beat in the icing (confectioners') sugar and cocoa. Beat really well until smooth and velvety. Slowly beat in the milk, adding a little more each time until you have a soft, spreadable icing.

When the cake is cold, smother the whole thing in the icing and artfully place a load of chocolate eggs on top. Try not to bury your face in the cake. Bad form.

Easter rabbit cake

Easter chicks, Easter eggs, Easter daffodils, Easter rabbits. Ah ha! Yes! And what do rabbits like to eat? Lettuce? Well, yes, but try again. Carrots? Why yes, carrots. So here is a cake, not made from rabbit (which would be nasty and a bit weird) but inspired by rabbits.

✳ Serves 10

175 g/6 oz/¾ cup soft light brown sugar

175 ml/6 fl oz/¾ cup sunflower oil

3 large free-range eggs

150 g/5 oz/1 ⅓ cups plain (all-purpose) flour

1 ½ tsp bicarbonate of soda (baking soda)

1 ½ tsp baking powder

1 tsp ground cinnamon

225 g/8 oz/1 ¼ cups grated carrots

50 g/1 ¾ oz/½ cup hazelnuts, roasted and chopped

50 g/1 ¾ oz/⅔ cup crystallized (candied) pineapple chunks, chopped

25 g/1 oz/1 ¾ tbsp unsalted butter

200 g/7 oz/1 ⅓ cup icing (confectioners') sugar, sifted

25 g/1 oz/1 ¾ tbsp cream cheese

150 g/5 oz white chocolate, melted

Easter decorations or sprinkles

Preheat the oven to 180°C/350°F/Gas mark 4. Grease and line a deep 20 cm/8 in tin (pan). In a large bowl, whisk together the brown sugar and oil, then add the eggs and whisk. Sift in the flour, bicarbonate of soda (baking soda), baking powder and cinnamon and carry on whisking. Next, stir in the grated carrots, hazelnuts and pineapple. Pour the mixture into the tin and bake for about 45 minutes until the top is springy and a knife or skewer comes out clean.

Cool the cake in its tin for 10 minutes before turning it onto a wire rack to become completely cold. Meanwhile, crack on with the icing. Cream together the butter and icing (confectioners') sugar – the mixture will be really stiff. Then carefully work in the cream cheese. Don't overdo it, because it can make the icing go runny. If it gets too thin, just add more icing sugar until the icing reaches the consistency of really thick porridge (but without the lumps). Stir in the melted white chocolate. If the mix is a little thin at this stage, pop the bowl in the fridge for 20 minutes or so – that'll get it to behave. Spread the icing over the cake and scatter with your chosen adornments.

Chocolate hazelnut cake

This is a spectacularly good cake if you love the combination of chocolate and hazelnuts. It's on a scrap of paper in my really untidy collection of recipes. I have a very strong feeling that it originated from Tamasin Day-Lewis, and would hate not to give her the credit for what is a truly delicious cake.

✳ Serves 8

175 g/6 oz/¾ cup unsalted butter

175 g/6 oz/¾ cup light soft brown sugar

3 large free-range eggs

2 tbsp milk

175 g/6 oz/1 ½ cups plain (all-purpose) flour

2 tsp baking powder

110 g/4 oz/1 ¼ cups ground hazelnuts

200 g/7 oz dark (bittersweet) chocolate (at least 70% cocoa solids), chopped into gravel-sized lumps

30 g/1 oz/¼ cup chopped hazelnuts

Preheat the oven to 160°C/325°F/Gas mark 3. Grease and line a 20 cm/8 in loose-bottomed tin (pan). Beat the butter and sugar together until really pale and creamy and then add the eggs one at a time, beating really well between each egg. Add the milk and give another thrashing before sifting in the flour and baking powder, followed by the ground hazelnuts and two-thirds of the chocolate. Fold everything in and, when it is well amalgamated, pop it into the tin. Smooth the top and then sprinkle over the rest of the chocolate and the chopped hazelnuts.

Bake for 1 hour and then you will need to cover the top of the cake with greaseproof paper (parchment paper) before giving the cake another 20–30 minutes. The centre of the cake will be firmly springy when it is done. Cool the cake for 10 minutes or so in the tin before carefully transferring it to a wire rack.

Boozy cherry and almond cake

This is basically a kirsch-soaked frangipane, studded with cherries. Gorgeous, in my world. You could easily make this into a tart by blind-baking a sweet pastry case and then piling the frangipane mixture into it and baking as normal.

✳ Serves 8

250 g/9 oz/1 cup plus 2 tbsp unsalted butter, softened

250 g/9 oz/1 ⅓ cups caster (superfine) sugar

25 g/1 oz/¼ cup plain (all-purpose) flour

250 g/9 oz/3 cups ground almonds

4 large free-range eggs

600 g/1 lb 5 oz can of dark cherries, stoned and drained

3–7 tbsp kirsch

3 tbsp apricot jam

Preheat the oven to 160°C/325°F/Gas mark 3. Grease and line a loose-bottomed 20 cm/8 in tin (pan) – a springform one is ideal, but there's no need to worry if you don't have one.

Cream the butter and sugar together until really pale and fluffy and then beat in the flour, followed by a tablespoon of the almonds. Then, one at a time, beat in the eggs. Finally, fold in the remaining almonds.

Spread the mixture in the tin and place the cherries on top – you don't need to prod them in as they will gently snuggle down in the developing cake as it rises. Bake for about 1 hour or until golden and splendid.

Take the beauty out of the oven, reserve 1 tablespoon kirsch from the allotted amount (which depends on how boozy you want it) and drizzle the rest over the warm cake. Leave it to cool in its tin. Meanwhile, put the jam in a small pan with the reserved kirsch and warm gently so that the jam liquefies and the kirsch blends in. Then, when the cake is barely warm, brush this glaze over the top and leave for another 1–2 hours before digging in.

Apricot and cardamom cake

One definitely for the adults, I think (unless your child has a super-sophisticated palette, that is). I love cardamom in both sweet and savoury food and I think it works really well with apricots. Although it would be gorgeous to use fresh apricots, it can be difficult to find them tasting of anything other than cotton wool. Behold the canned apricot. I have a feeling that the anti-margarine brigade will add this to their list of unmentionables. I refuse to apologize. They're lovely!

✳ Serves 10

1 x 410 g/14 oz can apricot halves in fruit juice (not syrup)

3 tsp cardamom pods

175 g/6 oz/¾ cup unsalted butter

110 g/4 oz/½ cup caster (superfine) sugar

3 large free-range eggs

200 g/7 oz/scant 2 cups self-raising flour

½ tsp bicarbonate of soda (baking soda)

50 g/1 ¾ oz/¼ cup polenta

3 tbsp thick natural yogurt (Greek, if possible)

2 tbsp runny honey

2 tbsp demerara sugar

Preheat the oven to 180°C/350°F/Gas mark 4. Grease and line a 20 cm/8 in loose-bottomed tin (pan). Drain the apricots really well and arrange them in the bottom of the tin in a single layer. Crack the cardamom pods open, scrape out the little black seeds and crush them in a pestle and mortar.

In a mixer, cream the butter and sugar until pale and fluffy and beat in the eggs one by one. Sift the flour and the bicarbonate of soda (baking soda) over the mixture, then add the cardamom powder and polenta and fold everything in. Finally, add the yogurt and carefully stir that in, too.

Pour the mixture over the apricots and carefully spread it out. Bake for about 45–60 minutes or until a knife or skewer comes out clean.

Leave the cake to cool for 10 minutes or so in the tin and then carefully invert it over a plate. If any apricots misbehave, just place them back with a prod. Mix together the honey and demerara and drizzle over the top of the cake.

Lemon polenta cake
with rosemary

Believe me, a lemony sugar syrup infused with rosemary poured over the cake turns this into a sublime experience.

❋ Serves 8

225 g/8 oz/1 cup unsalted butter, softened

225 g/8 oz/1 cup caster (superfine) sugar

225 g/8 oz/2 ⅔ cups ground almonds

3 large free-range eggs

zest and juice of 3 unwaxed lemons

110 g/4 oz/generous ½ cup polenta

½ tsp baking powder

80 g/2 ¾ oz/⅓ cup caster (superfine) sugar

2 sprigs of fresh rosemary, approx 4 cm/1 ½ in long

Preheat the oven to 160°C/325°F/Gas mark 3. Grease and line a 20 cm/8 in loose-bottomed tin (pan). Cream together the butter and sugar until pale and fluffy. Add a tablespoonful of the almonds and then beat in the eggs, one at a time, beating well between each egg. Fold in the remaining almonds and the lemon zest, along with the polenta and baking powder. Pop the mixture into the tin and bake for about 45 minutes or until a knife or skewer comes out clean.

While the cake is in the oven, prepare the syrup. Put the caster (superfine) sugar, lemon juice and rosemary into a small pan and bring to the boil. Boil for 2 minutes or until all the sugar has dissolved.

Cool the syrup a little and sieve it. When the cake is out of the oven, let it cool for 10 minutes or so in its tin. Poke about 20 holes in the cake and pour the syrup over so that it sinks into the holes. Leave the cake for a couple of hours to soak up all those lovely juices before removing it from the tin and serving.

A sophisticated cake

This is such a feminine cake – the idea of rosewater always makes me think of ladies with floaty dresses, genteel manners and a thorough working knowledge of the difficulties of maintaining a good herbaceous border. The cake is very easy and, although the crystallized (candied) roses may seem difficult, they really aren't – all they require is forward planning and access to some lovely fragrant old-fashioned roses.

✳ Serves 8

For the crystallized (candied) roses:

approx 4 large heavily scented rose heads (or 8 buds) that haven't been sprayed with toxic chemicals

2 large free-range egg whites

300 g/10 oz/1 ½ cups caster (superfine) sugar

For the cake:

4 large free-range eggs, separated

175 g/6 oz/¾ cup caster (superfine) sugar

225 g/8 oz/2 ⅔ cups ground almonds

½ tsp cream of tartar

¼ tsp bicarbonate of soda (baking soda)

1 tsp rosewater

grated zest and juice of 2 large unwaxed lemons

200 g/7 oz/1 ⅓ cups icing (confectioners') sugar, sifted

A day before you want to eat the cake, prepare the roses. Carefully separate the petals, gently rinse them and leave them to dry on paper towels. Gently whisk up the egg whites, just enough to loosen them. Pour the caster (superfine) sugar onto a large plate or tray and have ready another large tray or baking sheet, lined with silicone paper.

Take one dry petal and dip it into the egg white, ensuring that it is completely covered, then drop the petal into the sugar. I prefer to sprinkle more sugar on top at this stage rather than handle the petal too much. When it's covered in sugar, gently shake off the excess and lay it on the lined tray. Repeat with all the petals. Leave the petals to dry out in a warm place.

For the cake, preheat the oven to 180°C/350°F/Gas mark 4 and grease and line a 20 cm/8 in loose-bottomed cake tin (pan). Put the egg yolks and sugar into a bowl and beat with an electric whisk until the mixture is pale and thick. Wash the whisk really well, and in a second, very clean bowl, whisk the egg whites until they stand in stiff peaks. Fold the whites into the yolks and then fold in the almonds, cream of tartar, bicarbonate of soda (baking soda) and rosewater.

Bake for about 30 minutes, or until a knife or skewer comes out clean. You may need to protect the top of the cake with greaseproof paper (parchment paper) if it looks as if it's starting to scorch. Leave the cake to cool on a wire rack.

Make the icing by mixing the lemon juice with the icing (confectioners') sugar. The icing should be gorgeously sharp, but if you want to you could add a few drops of rosewater, too. I advise caution here; don't overdo it! The consistency should be like single cream. Spoon the icing over the cake so that it gently drips down the sides, and arrange the petals artfully on top. Leave the icing to set, then serve.

Elderflower cake

This is in fact courgette and elderflower cake, but it's best not to mention the courgette until the recipient has already tried a slice – it puts people off, I've discovered. Once they've eaten some of it, they'll just shrug their shoulders and carry on eating more.

✳ Serves 8–10

200 ml/7 fl oz/scant 1 cup sunflower oil

250 g/9 oz/1 ⅓ cups caster (superfine) sugar

3 large free-range eggs, separated

3 tbsp milk

150 g/5 oz courgette, grated

finely grated zest of 2 large unwaxed lemons

225 g/8 oz/2 cups self-raising flour, sifted

1 tsp baking powder

150 g/5 oz/⅔ cup unsalted butter, softened

100 g/3 ½ oz/scant ½ cup cream cheese

500 g/1 lb 2 oz/about 3 ¼ cups icing (confectioners') sugar, sifted

2 tbsp elderflower cordial

Preheat the oven to 160°C/325°F/Gas mark 3. Grease and line a 20 cm/8 in loose-bottomed cake tin (pan). Put the oil and the caster (superfine) sugar into a bowl and whisk away until they are well amalgamated. Then add the egg yolks, one by one, whisking well between each addition. Next, whisk in the milk and, when that has been incorporated, stir in the courgette and the zest of 1 lemon. Fold in the flour and the baking powder carefully. In another bowl, whisk the egg whites until really stiff and fold them into the mixture in three goes.

Put the mixture into the tin, level the surface and bake for about 30 minutes, or until a knife or skewer comes out clean. Keep an eye on the top of the cake and cover it with greaseproof paper (parchment paper) if it seems to be going a dark shade of brown ('burning', as it is also known). Cool the cake on a wire rack.

To make the icing, beat together the butter and cream cheese and add the icing (confectioners') sugar. Beat until the mixture is pale and fluffy and then add the elderflower cordial and remaining lemon zest and beat them in, too. Have a taste and add more lemon or elderflower if needed. The icing should have a gorgeous floral tang. If the icing is too runny, add more icing sugar, and if too thick, add more lemon juice or elderflower cordial.

When the cake is cold, spread the icing all over the top and let it creep down the sides, but don't worry too much about actively icing the sides. Although this cake is in the Posh section, I don't think it's mega-formal.

Sprinkle the top with nothing or anything, depending on your mood: chopped pistachios, a sprig of elderflower itself, a few of the tiniest silver balls or a smidgen of chopped angelica all work well.

Gâteau amandine

Right, if you're going to make this French delight properly, you should use a proper sloping-sided baking tin (pan). I don't have one – I make it in an ordinary cake tin. No one has ever complained and, as far as I am aware, it's not actually illegal. Especially if you're not French.

✳ Serves 8–10

3 large free-range eggs

125 g/4 ½ oz/⅔ cup caster (superfine) sugar

few drops of almond extract

75 g/2 ½ oz/scant ¾ cup plain (all-purpose) flour

300 ml/½ pt/1 cup double (whipping) cream

40 g/1 ¼ oz/3 ½ tbsp icing (confectioners') sugar, sifted

2 ½ tbsp almond liqueur

100 g/3 ½ oz/1 ¼ cups flaked almonds, toasted

Preheat the oven to 180°C/350°F/Gas mark 4. Grease and line a 24 cm/9 ½ in cake tin (pan), preferably loose-bottomed.

Put the eggs and caster (superfine) sugar into a large, heatproof bowl and place this bowl over a pan of barely simmering water, not letting the base of the bowl touch the water. With an electric whisk, beat the eggs and sugar until the mixture is really pale and thick and leaves a trail when you lift the whisk. Take the bowl off the heat, add the almond extract and keep on whisking until the mixture has cooled. Sift the flour over and carefully fold in. Pop the mixture into the tin and bake for about 30 minutes until golden brown and a knife or skewer inserted comes out cleanly. Cool the cake on a wire rack.

Whisk the cream with the icing (confectioners') sugar and almond liqueur until the mixture is softly thick. Do not overwhip the cream. Then spread it over the top and sides of the cake and sprinkle the flaked almonds all over it. Voilà.

Gâteau St. Honoré

Are you ready for this French fiesta of faff? I'm warning you, this is a total humdinger of an afternoon's work. This isn't meant to put you off – you can do a bit, wander off, feed the cat, come back, do a bit more, stare into the neighbour's garden for a while, come back – but no one will be left in any doubt about how much effort you have put in. This cake, apparently, is in honour of St. Honoré, the patron saint of bakers. Good man.

✳ Serves 8

For the pastry base:

100 g/3 ½ oz/scant 1 cup plain (all-purpose) flour

50 g/1 ¾ oz/scant ¼ cup caster (superfine) sugar

50 g/1 ¾ oz/scant ¼ cup unsalted butter

2 large free-range egg yolks

1 large free-range egg, beaten

For the choux buns:

50 g/1 ¾ oz/scant ¼ cup unsalted butter

150 ml/5 fl oz/⅔ plain (all-purpose) flour

2 large free-range eggs, beaten

For the crème patissière:

350 ml/12 fl oz/1 ½ cups milk

150 ml/5 fl oz/⅔ cup double (whipping) cream

1 vanilla pod

1 large free-range egg

3 large free-range egg yolks

75 g/2 ½ oz/¼ cup caster (superfine) sugar

45 g/1 ½ oz/scant ⅓ cup cornflour (cornstarch)

To finish:

300ml/10 fl oz/1 ¼ cups double (whipping) cream

50 g/1 ¾ oz/scant ¼ cup caster (superfine) sugar

2 tbsp water

First of all, make the base, which is essentially a sweet pastry. This is much easier if you use a food processor, although you can do it by hand. Put the flour, sugar and butter into the processor and whizz until you have fine crumbs. Add the egg yolks and blitz again until a lump of dough forms. You can add a splash of very cold water, if you need to. Take the dough out of the bowl, put it on a lightly floured work surface and give it a quick knead. Wrap the dough in cling film (plastic wrap) and pop it in the fridge for at least 30 minutes. Don't try to leave the refrigeration stage out. Never worth it. Tantrums, bad pastry.

After its rest, roll out the pastry on a floured surface until you have a circle of approximately 18 cm/7 in diameter. Put it onto a baking sheet, prick the surface all over with a fork, and pop it back in the fridge while you make the choux pastry. At this stage, preheat the oven to 190°C/375°F/Gas mark 5.

For the choux pastry, put the butter and water into a saucepan and bring to the boil. Remove the pan from the heat, quickly tip in all the flour and then, with a wooden spoon, beat the living daylights out of it. Really go for it – a proper expending of energy is required here. The contents of the pan should form a ball in the centre of the pan. Get your breath back and let the mixture cool for a minute or two.

For the next stage, I use an electric hand whisk, but you can continue with your workout if you wish and do it by hand. Very slowly, start beating in the eggs, little by little, until you have a lovely shiny mixture. Spoon the mixture into a piping (decorating) bag fitted with a 1 cm/½ in plain nozzle (tube).

Take the sweet pastry out of the fridge and brush around the outside of the circle with beaten egg, then pipe a ring of choux pastry over the egg. Brush the choux pastry with egg as well. On a separate baking sheet lined with silicone paper, pipe about 20 walnut-sized balls of choux pastry, remembering to leave plenty of room between each bun for spreadage. Brush the buns with egg, too.

Pop everything into the oven and bake for about 15 minutes until the buns and the choux ring are risen and golden. As soon as the buns are out of the oven, make a small slit in the side of each one to let the steam out. If they look very damp inside, pop them back in the oven for another 5 minutes.

Now the crème patissière: pour the milk and the cream into a

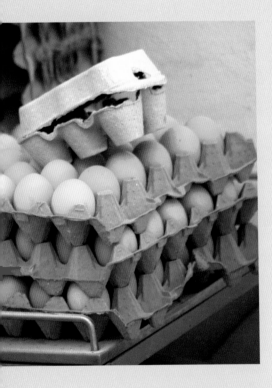

heavy-based saucepan, split the vanilla pod and, with the point of a sharp knife, scrape out all the seeds and plop them into the milk. Chuck in the pod for good measure and gently heat until the liquid comes almost to the boil. You want to see the very edges of the pan starting to sizzle. At this point, turn off the heat.

In a bowl, whisk the whole egg and egg yolks with the sugar until pale and fluffy. Add one third of the cornflour (cornstarch) and whisk until it's completely amalgamated. Keep going like this, a third at a time, until all the cornflour has been whisked in and the mixture is really smooth.

Fish the vanilla pod out of the milk and pour the milk over the egg and sugar mixture, whisking like fury as you go. Give the milk pan a quick wipe over and tip the custard back in. Gently heat the mixture, whisking continuously until it is deliciously thick and all floury traces have been cooked out. Tip the custard into a bowl and cover the surface with cling film to stop a skin forming.

Whip the cream until it is what I would confusingly call 'softly thick'. I think over-whipped cream is vile and like it on the softer side, but it's up to you. Using either a piping bag or simply a teaspoon, fill each of the individual choux buns with the whipped cream.

Make a caramel by heating the sugar and water in a pan and boiling until the sugar dissolves and turns a pale golden colour – don't overdo it. Dip the top of each of the choux buns in the caramel and then use a tiny dab more to stick the bun to the choux ring. You should now have a rather splendid wall of choux. Fill the centre of the whole shebang with the crème patissière and drizzle with any remaining caramel. Phew.

A posher coffee cake

Look, I know the appearance of margarine might seem a bit odd, but believe me, this cake is still posh. The mousseline which sandwiches the sponges together is an altogether grander affair than your normal buttercream. Will that do?

275 g/9 ½ oz/2 ⅔ cups self-raising flour, sifted

275 g/9 ½ oz/scant 1 ½ cups caster (superfine) sugar

275 g/9 ½ oz/1 ¼ cups soft margarine

5 large free-range eggs

4 tbsp instant coffee granules, made up with 1 ½ tbsp boiling water

For the mousseline:

60 g/2 oz/scant ⅓ cup caster (superfine) sugar

4 tbsp water

2 large free-range egg yolks

150 g/5 oz/⅔ cup unsalted butter, softened

chocolate coffee beans, to decorate

Preheat the oven to 160°C/325°F/Gas mark 3. Grease and line three 20 cm/8 in sandwich tins (pans).

In a mixer, beat together the flour, sugar, margarine, eggs and half of the strong coffee mixture. Beat away until pale and fluffy and then divide it between the three tins and smooth out the mixture. Bake for 20–25 minutes until golden and springy to the touch. Turn out the cakes onto a wire rack to cool.

To make the mousseline, put the sugar and water into a pan, bring to the boil and boil for about 10 minutes until it reaches 105°C (220°F) on a sugar thermometer. For those without one, you want the syrup to reach the thread stage – it forms a thread when you press it between your thumb and finger, but please be careful! Whisk the egg yolks in a bowl and slowly add the syrup in a steady stream, whisking all the time. Then whisk in the butter, followed by the coffee mixture left over from the cake. Have a taste. Add a bit more coffee, if you want.

Sandwich the three cakes together with the mousseline and then spread more over the top. Finally, scatter some chocolate coffee beans over.

Chocolate truffle cake

Not for the fainthearted, this one. A pure slice of chocolate heavenliness. The sort of cake that if you eat too much leaves you feeling a little bit dirty – always a sign of a really great chocolate cake.

✳ Serves 8

175 g/6 oz/¾ cup unsalted butter, softened

350 g/12 oz/1 ¾ cups caster (superfine) sugar

1 tsp vanilla extract

3 large free-range eggs

175 ml/6 fl oz/¾ cup milk

300 ml/½ pt/1 ¼ cups sour cream

75 g/2 ½ oz/scant ¾ cup plain (all-purpose) flour, sifted

150 g/5 oz/1 ⅓ cups self-raising flour, sifted

100 g/3 ½ oz/¾ cup cocoa powder

600 ml/1 pt/2 cups double (whipping) cream

400 g/14 oz dark (bittersweet) chocolate (at least 70% cocoa solids), chopped into chunks

200 g/7 oz milk chocolate, chopped into chunks

Preheat the oven to 180°C/350°F/Gas mark 4. Grease and line a 20 cm/8 in loose-bottomed tin (pan).

In a mixer (preferably), beat the butter and sugar together until pale and fluffy and then beat in the vanilla. Add the eggs, one at a time, beating well before adding the next. Then beat in the milk and sour cream – don't worry about the curdled effect. Sift over the plain and self-raising flours and cocoa and gently fold them in. Tip the mixture into the prepared tin and smooth it out. Make a slight indent in the centre with the back of a spoon and then bake for about 1 hour, or until a knife or skewer inserted comes out clean.

Cool the cake in the tin for 10 minutes before turning onto a wire rack. While the cake is cooling, make the ganache. Pour the double (whipping) cream into a heavy-based pan and slowly heat it to just below simmering point (you want bubbles on the base of the pan if you tip it, but not actually on the surface). Take the pan off the heat and chuck the chocolate into the cream. Leave them to get to know each other for a minute or two and then gently stir everything together so that all the chocolate melts. Leave the pan alone until the ganache has turned into a thick, soft, spreadable paste.

When the cake is cold and the ganache has stiffened, split the cake into two and sandwich it back together with a spoon or two of the ganache. Then, using a palette knife, carefully plaster the whole shebang in the ganache. Top, sides, the lot. Decorate the top of the cake with anything you feel appropriately decadent – I love a silver almond, myself.

Upside-down pineapple and salted caramel cake

The salted caramel and pineapple combination originated from Vicky Bhogal, an amazing cookery writer I met a while ago. She introduced me to the idea of frying fruit in butter. Oh Vicky, what have you started? Traditional upside-down cake is an amazingly kitsch affair and so appeals, of course.

✳ Serves 8

125g/4 ½ oz/½ cup plus 1 tbsp butter

450 g/1 lb/2 ¾ cups caster (superfine) sugar

1 large pineapple, peeled, cored and sliced

200 g/7 oz/scant 2 cups plain (all-purpose) flour

1 tsp baking powder

¼ tsp bicarbonate of soda (baking soda)

2 large free-range eggs

75 ml/2 ½ fl oz/scant ⅓ cup sunflower oil

200 ml/7 fl oz/scant 1 cup buttermilk

1 tsp vanilla extract

160 ml/5 ½ fl oz/scant ¾ cup double (whipping) cream

1–2 tsp coarse sea salt

Preheat the oven to 160°C/325°F/Gas mark 3. Grease and line a 20 cm/8 in loose-bottomed tin (pan) – springform if you have one.

Melt 50 g/1 ¾ oz/scant ¼ cup butter in a pan and stir in 150 g/5 oz/⅔ cup caster (superfine) sugar. Heat gently for about 2 minutes. Put this gloopy mixture into the prepared tin and place the pineapple in an even layer on top, making sure that there are no holes in the pineapple layer.

Sift the flour, baking powder and bicarbonate of soda (baking soda) into a large bowl. In another bowl or a jug, mix together 150 g/5 oz/⅔ cup caster sugar, the eggs, oil and buttermilk. Whisk this mixture into the dry ingredients and then pour onto the pineapple in the tin. Bake for about 30 minutes or until the cake is firm and springy to the touch.

While the cake is in the oven, make the salted caramel sauce. Put the remaining caster sugar into a heavy-based pan and heat gently. Don't stir it. Please don't. The caramel will crystallize and go yucky. When the sugar has dissolved and turned a light amber colour, carefully add the cream – it will splutter and spit. Then stir in the remaining butter and, as soon as it has melted, take the sauce off the heat. Let the sauce cool to just below lava stage before even attempting to try it. This stuff is hotter than a hot day in hell.

Take your mind off the sauce by turning the cake out of the tin. Place a plate over the top of the tin and flip it over before removing the tin and greaseproof paper (parchment paper). Spoon any juices that escape back over the top of the cake.

Stir a teaspoon of crunchy salt into the sauce and carefully try it. Add more if you like it saltier. When you are happy, pour the sauce over the cake, keeping back any extra and serving separately with the cake. Yummy.

Little cakes

Small things hold a curious fascination for me. I can quite see how people become obsessed with doll's houses. I thought I loved a good doll's house, but, in fact, what I really love is the stuff inside – the ordinariness of life shrunk beyond belief. Nothing in that house could be more fascinating than the food. I get quite excited just thinking about the baskets of tiny cabbages and carrots, the lump of cheese, the platter with a boiled ham (there is always a boiled ham) and, of course, the cakes. I could stare at this stuff all day.

I like small food in the real world, too. If I could live my life just eating canapés, I would be thrilled. I'd eat a lot of them, you understand; this isn't about some weird sort of portion control. I just like the size of them. Miniature sandwiches, sausages, Yorkshire puddings, blinis – yes please. Don't even get me started on the sweet stuff. Oh, go on, then. Get me started.

Small cakes are a delight to behold. Not only are they perfect for those mid-morning and mid-afternoon occasions, they are so aesthetically pleasing. It's almost impossible to make them look ugly. One cherry bun might look a bit sad on its own, but a dozen or so of them piled up look like art to me.

My proudest moment of this chapter has to be the fondant fancy. There really can't be many people who don't have fond memories of these wonders. The cherry bun recipe might seem a bit odd, but it's crucial that it appears. This is the recipe that I first cooked on my own as a child – with no help at all, with the oven or anything. As a result, I made these a great deal. This is the recipe that introduced me not only to baking, but cooking.

If you are planning to do some baking with a juvenile-type person, may I suggest baking some little cakes as a starting point? You don't have to make cherry cakes – go with the flow and create a mountain of small morsels that satisfy all concerned.

For me, little cakes are wondrous things that bridge the gap between doll's-house-food heaven and actual-edible heaven. Who could ask for more?

Chocolate brownies

Chocolate, walnuts, gooey, squidgy, sweet and criminally easy. Surely some form of miracle cake?

✷ Makes about 18

110 g/4 oz/½ cup unsalted butter

50 g/1 ¾ oz dark (bittersweet) chocolate (at least 70% cocoa solids)

2 large free-range eggs, lightly beaten

225 g/8 oz/1 cup caster (superfine) sugar

50 g/1 ¾ oz/scant ½ cup plain (all-purpose) flour, sifted

100 g/3 ½ oz/1 cup walnuts, chopped

Preheat the oven to 180°C/350°F/Gas mark 4. Grease and line a tin (pan) about 18 x 28 cm/7 x 11 in – I use a small Swiss roll (jelly roll) tin.

Pop a heatproof bowl over a pan of barely simmering water, but don't let the bottom of the bowl touch the water. Melt the butter and chocolate in the bowl. Take the pan off the heat and let the mixture cool for about 5 minutes, then tip it into a bigger bowl, add all the other ingredients and give it a good old beat with a wooden spoon.

Pour the mixture into the prepared tin and level the surface. Bake for about 30 minutes. The top will have crisped over but the middle will still be soggy – don't be afraid to take it out of the oven as it continues to set as it cools. There's nothing worse than an overcooked brownie; you want a decent squidge. Leave it to cool in the tin before cutting it up and transferring to your mouth. Quality control is imperative.

Meringues

I love this recipe. It's my Mum's. She makes the best meringues. I love her recipe because of the lack of ingredients, lack of techniques and lack of general fuss. The key here is slow cooking. I mean, really slow. Slower than a slug with a limp having a bad day. That slow.

✳ Makes about 8 big
  billowy meringues or
  18–20 delicate ones

4 large free-range egg whites

225 g/8 oz/1 cup caster
  (superfine) sugar

Preheat the oven to its lowest-ever setting. Barely warm is good. Line a couple of baking sheets with silicone paper. Top tip: ordinary greaseproof paper (parchment paper) will not do; it will stick like glue and there will be tears. Silicone paper or the reuseable liners are what you are after here.

In a scrupulously clean bowl, whisk the egg whites until they are stiff and then slowly whisk in half the caster (superfine) sugar. When the mixture is glossy and thick, fold in the remaining sugar.

At this stage you need to decide whether you are going big or small. If big, take two large spoons and form roughly oval shapes, then carefully plop them onto the sheets. Alternatively, spoon the mixture into a piping (decorating) bag fitted with a plain nozzle (tube) and pipe small meringues directly onto the silicone paper. You can make them as generous or as tiny as you like.

Bake the meringues for at least 2 hours. I often turn off the oven and go out, leaving them to it. You'll know when they're done as you'll be able to easily remove them from the lining, and the underside won't look marshmallowy. These beauties keep for weeks in an airtight tin.

Raspberry friands

Gorgeous fruity, spongey little cakes – they work well with lots of different soft fruits. Blackberries and blueberries are particularly delicious.

✳ Makes 12

175 g/6 oz/¾ cup unsalted butter

140 g/4 ¾ oz/1 ⅔ cups ground almonds

grated zest of 1 unwaxed lemon

280 g/10 oz/2 cups plus 2 tbsp icing (confectioners') sugar, sifted

2 large free-range egg whites

125 g/4 ½ oz/½ cup plus 1 tbsp plain (all-purpose) flour, sifted

200 g/7 oz raspberries

Preheat the oven to 180°C/350°F/Gas mark 4 and grease 12 bun tins (pans) – the shallow ones are best. Melt the butter and leave to cool. Put all the dry ingredients into a large bowl and stir well. Add the egg whites, followed by the butter, and give it all a good stir. Spoon the mixture into the tins and scatter the raspberries over the top. Bake for about 15 minutes or until golden and springy to the touch. Cool them on a wire rack.

Macaroons

Macaroons make me smile. I love their garish colours, their unusual flavours, their crisp outer and squidgy inner. I also love the fact that they're gone in two mouthfuls, so you can legitimately have quite a few without looking excessively greedy. I've given you the basic version here, and it's up to you to add whatever flavours take your fancy. I make them with rosewater, lavender, lime, mandarin, lemon and bergamot.

✳ Makes about 20
   (10 with filling)

175 g/6 oz/1 ⅓ cups icing
   (confectioners') sugar

125 g/4 ½ oz/1 ½ cups ground
   almonds

3 large free-range egg whites

80 g/2 ¾ oz/⅓ cup caster
   (superfine) sugar

2–3 drops of flavouring
   (optional)

food colouring (optional)

75 g/2 ½ oz/¼ cup plus
   1 tbsp unsalted butter,
   softened

150 g/5 oz/1 cup plus
   2 tbsp icing (confectioners')
   sugar, sifted

Preheat the oven to 160°C/325°F/Gas mark 3 and line two baking sheets with silicone liners. In a food processor, blitz the icing (confectioners') sugar and the ground almonds. I know they are already ground, but this extra milling makes all the difference. Then sieve the mixture into a large bowl. Discard any chunky bits that remain in the sieve.

In another bowl, whisk the egg whites until really stiff and then whisk in the caster (superfine) sugar until you have a glossy meringue. Add the food colouring and the flavouring to the meringue and continue to whisk.

Then, very carefully (I do this in three goes), fold the meringue into the dry ingredients and continue folding until the mixture leaves a ribbon trail. Carefully spoon the mixture into a piping (decorating) bag fitted with a plain nozzle (tube) and pipe small blobs (about 2.5 cm/1 in across) onto the trays, leaving a good gap between each macaroon.

Next is the crucial bit. It's not often I get really strict, but listen up: leave the macaroons to dry out in the air until they form a skin. Do not, do you hear me, attempt to bake them while they are tacky to the touch. This may take 10 minutes, it may take 45. It really does depend on the humidity of the surroundings.

Have they formed a skin? Yes? Good, let's move on. Pop them in the oven for 15 minutes or so. They're done when you can gently prod them along the liner. Not budging? Probably not done yet. When you're happy, take them out and carefully put them on a wire rack to cool.

Make the buttercream filling by beating the butter and the icing sugar together. Add colour and flavour to match the macaroons and, when they are cool, sandwich them together, pile them up and marvel at your brilliance.

Millefeuille

An impossible cake to eat elegantly. To be honest, you may as well just pick it up in two hands and push it into your mouth (but I bet you won't). This cake is a right old show-off and jolly delicious to eat, too, but here's the thing: it's a doddle to make. Swap the fruit around as you wish. The jam is an optional extra. This is one of those cakes that's just asking to be mucked about with.

✳ Serves 6

500 g/1 lb 2 oz packet of all-butter puff pastry

5 tbsp icing (confectioners') sugar, sifted, plus extra for dusting (optional)

300 ml/10 fl oz/1 ¼ cups double (whipping) cream

1 vanilla pod

1 tbsp caster (superfine) sugar

6 tsp raspberry jam (optional)

350 g/12 oz strawberries, raspberries or any other soft fruit

Preheat the oven to 200°C/400°F/Gas mark 6. Roll out the pastry on a floured surface, trying to keep it rectangular if you can, until it is about 5 mm/¼ in thick. Then, with a sharp knife and a steady hand, cut it into nine rectangles about twice as long as they are wide. Place them on a greased and floured baking sheet and sprinkle the icing (confectioners') sugar over the top of the raw pastry. Bake for about 15 minutes or until the pastry is puffy and golden. Cool the rectangles on a wire rack while you get on with the cream.

Whisk the cream until it reaches the floppy soft-peak stage. Make a slit down the entire length of the vanilla pod, scrape out the seeds with the point of the knife and transfer them to the cream. Sprinkle the caster (superfine) sugar over as well, and carry on whipping until you get a stiffer consistency. Don't overdo it, though – you don't want butter.

Slice the strawberries if you're using them; smaller fruit can be left whole. Carefully split each piece of pastry into two so that you end up with 18 rectangles of pastry, nine with glazed tops and nine looking a bit peaky. Because I cannot be trusted at times like these, I always put six of the nicest-looking glazed tops to one side to make sure that I don't use them in the middle of the building process.

Spread half a teaspoon of jam over a piece of pastry, top it with some cream and some fruit and place another piece of pastry on top. Repeat the process and finish with one from the 'nice' pile. Carry on until you have done all six. You can dust the top with more icing sugar if you like – and if you are feeling really snazzy, you can brand them with heated metal skewers to make lovely markings on the top.

Profiteroles

Choux pastry sounds terrifying, but really isn't. If you have an electric hand whisk, or a freestanding mixer, it's a complete cinch. Who can resist a profiterole?

✳ Serves 8

100 g/3 ½ oz/scant ½ cup unsalted butter

300 ml/10 fl oz/1 ¼ cups water

125/4 ½ oz/1 ¼ cups plain (all-purpose) flour

4 large free-range eggs, beaten

300 ml/10 fl oz/1 ¼ cups double (whipping) cream, whipped

For the sauce:

150 g/5 oz dark (bittersweet) chocolate, broken into small chunks.

150 ml/5 fl oz/⅔ cup double (whipping) cream

50 g/1 ¾ oz/scant ¼ cup unsalted butter

Preheat the oven to 220°C/425°F/Gas mark 7 and line two baking sheets, preferably with silicone liners. Put the butter and water into a saucepan and heat until the butter has melted, then bring up to the boil. Take the pan off the heat and quickly plonk the flour straight in. Now get a wooden spoon and start beating the living daylights out of it until the mixture forms a ball in the middle of the pan, then return the pan to the heat and continue beating until the mixture is smooth. That's the hard work done.

Take the pan off the heat and let the mixture cool a bit. Either with a handheld electric whisk in the saucepan or with the mixture in a freestanding mixer, start beating the eggs slowly into the mixture. Keep beating until the mixture takes on a lovely glossy sheen.

Put the mixture into a piping (decorating) bag fitted with a plain nozzle (tube) and pipe about 20 buns onto the baking sheets. Bake for about 20 minutes or until all puffed up and golden. Take them out of the oven and lower the temperature to 180°C/350°F/Gas mark 4. Make a small slit in the side of each bun to let the steam escape and pop them back in the oven for 5 minutes. Then take them out and cool them on a wire rack.

Just before you are ready to eat them, spoon or pipe some of the whipped cream into each bun and arrange them in a mountain of loveliness. Make the sauce by heating the cream until it just comes up to simmering point and taking it off the heat straight away. Put the chocolate and the butter into the cream and leave for a couple of moments before gently stirring everything until it all melts and blends into the most heavenly sauce. Pour some over the choux mountain and put the rest in a jug for the greedy so and so's who inevitably will want more.

French madeleines

Ah, bonjour! We have now left English 'cake' behind and are submerged in the world of Proust and delicate, stylish morsels. You really do need proper madeleine moulds for these. Even I wouldn't make do with an alternative. These are a world apart from the coconut and jam combo. Definitely more Chanel suit than boiler suit.

✳ Makes about 15

60 g/2 oz/¼ cup unsalted butter, melted

1 large free-range egg

50 g/1 ¾ oz/scant ¼ cup caster (superfine) sugar

50 g/1 ¾ oz/scant ½ cup plain (all-purpose) flour

1 tsp vanilla extract

grated zest of 1 orange

icing (confectioners') sugar, for dusting

Preheat the oven to 180°C/350°F/Gas mark 4 and liberally grease the madeleine moulds. This is key if you want the madeleines to come out in one piece, and melted butter is just the job. Lots of it. Set aside the rest of the butter to cool – you need to measure out 3 tablespoons so, if you don't have it, melt a tad more.

Whisk the egg and sugar until really thick and fluffy and the whisk leaves a ribbon trail when you lift it. Then sift the flour directly over the egg and sugar and fold it in really gently. Add the vanilla and orange zest and fold these in, followed by the cool melted butter.

Fill each mould half full and bake for 8 minutes until the madeleines are golden and firm to the touch. Turn onto a wire rack to cool, and dust with icing (confectioners') sugar just before serving.

English madeleines

I say 'English' because the previous recipe was for French Madeleines and they really couldn't be more different. I make these when I need a blitz of borderline comedy in the cake department. They are ridiculous, if we are honest, but do taste good, which is the important thing. You are meant to use dariole moulds to get the right shape, but of course I don't have any and really don't have a call for them in my life. As you can see from the picture, I use little pudding basins that make them look even more ridiculous.

✳ Makes 8 in pudding basins (probably 10 in dariole moulds)

100 g/3 ½ oz/scant ½ cup unsalted butter

100 g/3 ½ oz/scant ½ cup caster (superfine) sugar

2 large free-range eggs, lightly beaten

100 g/3 ½ oz/scant 1 cup self-raising flour, sifted

3 tbsp strawberry jam, sieved

75 g/2 ½ oz/1 cup desiccated coconut

8–10 glacé (candied) cherries

Preheat the oven to 160°C/325°F/Gas mark 3 and grease your chosen moulds. I like to line the base with a disc of greaseproof paper (parchment paper) too, just to be on the safe side.

Beat the butter and the sugar together until really pale and fluffy and slowly beat in the eggs, a little at a time. Then fold in the flour. Spoon the mixture into the moulds and bake for about 20 minutes, or until springy and firm to the touch. Leave them in their moulds for 5 minutes before turning them out onto a wire tray to cool. If they're being stubborn, run a knife along the edge of the moulds and give them a good sharp tap on the bottom.

When the cakes are properly cold, slice off the tops so that they have a very flat base when you turn them upside down. Brush the jam over the whole cakes and cover in the coconut. I favour the throw-it-on approach; I put the coconut in a deep, wide dish, place the cakes on top of the coconut and sling small handfuls of coconut at the side and the top. Works for me, anyway. Top with a cherry and place on a retro doily to serve.

Rock buns

Ah, rock buns; the key element to any decent fête, school cake sale, or homemade cake competition. You really can't beat them. Rock-like in appearance, but not in texture, all hail the unsung hero of small cakes. Cup of tea obligatory and I like a whopper of a rock cake. A boulder, I suppose. So the numbers specified are entirely unreliable but based upon what I would sneeringly consider a 'normal' size. Shudder.

✴ Makes 12

225 g/8 oz/2 cups plain (all-purpose) flour

2 tsp baking powder

100 g/3 ½ oz/scant ½ cup unsalted butter

75 g/2 ½ oz/¾ cup demerara sugar, plus 2 tbsp

75 g/2 ½ oz/⅓ cup mixed dried fruit

grated zest of 1 unwaxed lemon

1 large free-range egg

1–2 tbsp milk

Preheat the oven to 180°C/350°F/Gas mark 4 and grease and line two baking sheets. Sift the flour and baking powder into a bowl and then rub in the butter so that the mixture resembles breadcrumbs. Add the 75 g/2 ½ oz/¾ cup of demerara sugar, the mixed fruit and the lemon zest and give it a good old stir. Add the egg and 1 tablespoon of the milk and mix until you have a stiff, but moist dough. Add the remaining milk if you need to.

Grab two forks and form rock-like shapes in heaps on the baking tray – this is where you get to make stones, rocks or boulders. Sprinkle the 2 tablespoons of demerara sugar over the top of your buns and bake for about 20 minutes or until they are golden brown. Cool on a wire rack and then quickly dash to the competition.

Buttermilk scones

Scones are the most incredible weapon to have in your armoury of instant cakes. They take 5 minutes to make, less than 10 minutes to bake and leaving them for 3 minutes to cool helps mildly. That means that when people turn up for tea, you can actually have these on the table as soon as your unexpected guests start turning their minds toward a cup of something and a digestive from the tin. To be able to produce a scone so evidently homemade, warm and fragrant will ensure that they leave your house in a state of awe.

✳ Makes 8

200 g/7 oz/scant 2 cups
    self-raising flour

50 g/1 ¾ oz/scant ¼ cup
    unsalted butter

grated zest of 1 lemon

20 g/¾ oz/1 ½ tbsp light
    muscovado sugar

100 g/3 ½ oz/⅔ cup raisins

75 ml/2 ½ fl oz/scant ⅓ cup
    buttermilk

1 large free-range egg,
    lightly beaten

Preheat the oven to 220°C/425°F/Gas mark 7. Rub the butter into the flour (I don't bother sieving it) until it resembles breadcrumbs. Pop the lemon zest, the sugar and the raisins in and stir it all about, then add the buttermilk and mix until it forms a soft dough. Tip it out onto a floured surface and knead the dough until it is smooth. Roll it out until it is about 2 cm/¾ in thick and then cut out rounds with a 5 cm/2 in cutter.

Place the scones on a greased baking sheet and brush with the beaten egg. Bake for 8–10 minutes or until risen and golden. They are delicious eaten warm with a good dollop of butter and jam.

Cheese and chilli scones

Oooh, I love a cheese scone. Recently I have developed a rather serious chilli habit. I blame the endorphins. Anyway, I was making cheese scones the other day and stuck my head in the fridge to look for the cheese when a green chilli seemed to call to me. Before I knew it, I had chopped up that chilli and chucked it into the scone dough. The chilli was right. And I was right to listen to its call.

✳ Makes 8–10

225 g/8 oz/2 cups plain (all-purpose) flour

1 tsp baking powder

40 g/1 ½ oz/3 tbsp unsalted butter

100 g/3 ½ oz/¾ cup strong Cheddar, finely grated

1 tsp mustard powder

1 green chilli, deseeded and finely chopped

150 ml/5 fl oz/⅔ cup milk

Preheat the oven to 200°C/400°F/Gas mark 6. Sift the flour and baking powder into a bowl, then rub in the butter until the mixture resembles fine breadcrumbs. Stir in half the cheese, the mustard powder, the chilli and about two-thirds of the milk. Stir until it forms a soft, light dough, adding more milk if you need to.

On a floured surface, roll out the dough to about 2 cm/¾ in thick and with a 5 cm/2 in cutter, cut out the scones. Place them on a baking tray, brush them with a little milk and sprinkle the remaining cheese on top.

Bake them for 8–10 minutes until risen, golden and utterly irresistible. Cool on a wire rack. Delicious with a bit more cheese and some mango chutney.

Jammy doughnuts

I do not own a deep-fat fryer. If I did, I would want to fry absolutely everything, so it really is better if I don't have one to start with. The thought of having an open pan of boiling fat on the stove terrifies me. I would knock it over, or set the place on fire – and my hair would smell. So that's not happening. But I do love doughnuts. What to do, what to do? Bake them, that's what. These really taste like doughnuts and are almost good for you because they are baked not fried. Hurrah!

✳ Makes 12

200 g/7 oz/2 cups strong white bread flour

¼ tsp salt

245 g/8 ½ oz/scant 1 ¼ cup caster (superfine) sugar

25 g/¾ oz/1 ½ tbsp butter

7 g/¼ oz easy blend yeast

5 tbsp milk

1 large free-range egg, beaten

4 tbsp strawberry jam (or jam of your choice)

50 g/1 ¾ oz/⅓ cup icing (confectioners') sugar

Put the flour and salt and 45 g/1 ½ oz/scant ¼ cup of the sugar into a big bowl and rub in the butter until it looks like fine breadcrumbs, then stir in the yeast. Heat the milk until it is warm – so you can easily leave your finger in it without shrieking. Mix the milk and the egg into the flour mixture until it forms a dough.

Flour a worktop (I like to have a pile of extra flour to one side, too) and tip the dough onto the worktop. Knead the dough until it stops being sticky (keep flouring your hands and adding a smidgen to the worktop) and keep going until the dough changes from being a bit rough under your fingers to beautifully smooth and elastic. Believe me, you'll know when you get there.

Put the dough back in the bowl and cover it with a tea towel. Leave in a warm place for about 1 hour or until doubled in size.

Take the dough out and give it another knead for a couple of minutes, then cut it into 12 equal pieces. Roll each ball out to a circle of about 10 cm/4 in and put a smallish teaspoon of jam right in the middle. Gather up the edges of the circle around the jam and pinch it all together to make a seal. Place the filled doughnut seal-side down on a baking tray and repeat the process, leaving lots of space between each one. Cover again with the tea towel and leave to prove once more for about 45 minutes.

Preheat the oven to 180°C/350°F/Gas mark 4 and bake the doughnuts for about 10 minutes or until beautifully golden. Cool them for a minute or so while you make the glaze. Mix the icing (confectioners') sugar with enough water to make a thin, runny, icing and brush each doughnut with it. Put the caster (superfine) sugar in a deep dish and roll the wet doughnuts in it. Lovely.

The fondant fancy

Very few cakes get the consistent reaction that I get with these. And it's a good reaction. Make these and a Battenburg and grown men will weep at your feet.

✳ Makes about 20

175 g/6 oz/¾ cup soft margarine

175 g/6 oz/1 ½ cups self-raising flour, sifted

175 g/6 oz/¾ cup caster (superfine) sugar

3 large free-range eggs

1 ½ tsp vanilla extract

75 g/2 ½ oz/¼ cup plus 1 tbsp unsalted butter, softened

350 g/12 oz/2 ⅔ cups icing (confectioners') sugar, sifted

food colouring

Preheat the oven to 160°C/325°F/Gas mark 3. Grease and line a 22 cm/8 ½ in square cake tin (pan). Put the margarine, flour, caster (superfine) sugar, eggs and 1 tablespoon vanilla into a freestanding mixer and beat until the mixture is light and fluffy. Pour it into the tin and bake for about 20 minutes or until firm and springy to the touch and a knife or skewer comes out cleanly. Cool the sponge on a wire rack.

Meanwhile, make the buttercream. Cream together the butter and 150 g/5 oz/1 cup plus 2 tbsp icing (confectioners') sugar with the remaining vanilla until really pale and creamy. You may need to add a drop of milk if the mixture is really stiff – you need to be able to pipe this stuff. Put the buttercream into a piping (decorating) bag fitted with a plain nozzle (tube).

Cut the cold cake into squares and pipe a small blob of buttercream into the centre of each cake. Let the buttercream dry for a minute or two while you make the icing. Mix a small amount of water into the remaining icing sugar until you have an icing that thickly coats the back of a spoon. If it is too runny, add more icing sugar; too thick, add a drop more water. Tint the icing whatever colour you like.

Put the cakes on a wire rack over a tray and spoon the icing over the top of each cake so that it runs down the sides. You may need to tease it over the corners, but let the icing do the work for you. Leave the fancies to dry on their rack for about an hour. Make up a little more icing if you wish and drizzle a contrasting zigzag line across each cake. You can do this directly off a spoon or with a piping (decorating) bag.

Now, square cake cases don't appear to exist. Lay out the required number of round cupcake cases (baking cups) and open them out a bit. Place each cake in a case and wrap the edges of the cases round the cakes. If you do this while the icing is slightly tacky, it will stick.

Jaffa cakes

There is a modicum of effort and forward planning here, but they are an absolute hoot and seem to make people shout 'jaffa cakes!' at you as if you didn't know what you had just made.

✳ Makes about 16

1 x 135 g/5 oz packet orange jelly

3 large free-range eggs

100 g/3 ½ oz/scant ½ cup caster (superfine) sugar

75 g/2 ½ oz/scant ¾ cup plain (all-purpose) flour, sifted

300 g/10 oz dark (bittersweet) chocolate (at least 70% cocoa solids)

75 g/2 ½ oz/¼ cup plus 1 tbsp unsalted butter

Line an 18 cm/7 in tin (pan) with two layers of cling film (plastic wrap), letting it hang over the edges. Make the jelly according to the instructions on the packet, but only make it up to half the volume (275 ml/9 fl oz/1 cup plus 2 tbsp). Pour the jelly into the tin and chill until set really firm.

Preheat the oven to 160°C/325°F/Gas mark 3 and grease and line a 22 cm/8 ½ in tin – I used a square one. Make the sponge by putting the eggs and the caster (superfine) sugar in a bowl over a pan of barely simmering water. Whisk until the mixture has doubled in volume and is very pale and thick, and the whisk leaves a ribbon trail on the surface of the mixture. Take the bowl off the heat and continue whisking for about 5 minutes until the mixture has cooled down. Sift the flour over the mix and carefully fold in. Spoon the mixture into the prepared tin, trying not to knock out any of the air as you go. Bake for about 20 minutes or until golden and firm to the touch. Cool the sponge on a wire rack.

When the cake is cold, using a 6 cm/2 ½ in cutter, cut rounds out of the cake and place on one side. Then take the jelly out of the fridge, turn it out of its tin and peel off the cling film. Cut out smaller rounds from the jelly – I used a 4 cm/1 ½ in egg cup as a cutter – and place a circle of jelly in the centre of each cake.

Place the chocolate and the butter in a heatproof bowl over a pan of barely simmering water, making sure it doesn't touch the base of the bowl. Let the two melt slowly and gently stir to amalgamate everything. Put the cakes on a wire rack set over a tray, spoon the melted chocolate over the jelly and cake and let it drizzle down the sides. Leave the cakes to set on the tray before gently prising them off and amazing your friends.

Lady Helene's towers

I have ruthlessly taken my friend Helen's roulade sponge and turned it into a different cake. Helen has seen, scoffed and given it her stamp of approval. Phew. The chocolate custard in the cake is a couple of spoonfuls sneaked from the bowl waiting for the Chocolate Meringue Tower (p.75). If you don't want to make a large quantity of custard, you could easily substitute whipped cream and the cake would be just as scrumptious.

✳ Makes 8 towers

175 g/6 oz dark (bittersweet) chocolate (at least 70% cocoa solids)

6 large free-range eggs, separated

175 g/6 oz/¾ cup caster (superfine) sugar

2 tbsp chocolate custard (p.75)

2 tbsp double (whipping) cream

100 ml/3 ½ fl oz/scant ½ cup double (whipping) cream, whipped

40 raspberries

icing (confectioners') sugar for dusting

Preheat the oven to 180°C/350°F/Gas mark 4. Grease and line a Swiss roll (jelly roll) tin (pan). Melt the chocolate in a bowl set over a pan of simmering water and let it cool slightly.

In the bowl, whisk the egg yolks and sugar together until very pale and fluffy. In another bowl, whisk the egg whites until stiff. Pour the chocolate into the egg yolk mixture, whisking as you do so, then fold the egg whites into the chocolate mixture in three goes. Pour the mixture into the prepared tin and bake for about 15 minutes, or until a knife or skewer comes out cleanly. Cool the cake in the tin. When the cake is cold, cut out 16 rounds with a 5 cm/2 in cutter and leave to one side.

In a clean bowl, beat the chocolate custard with the unwhipped cream to loosen it and then fold in the whipped cream. Spoon a small amount of the chocolate cream onto a round of sponge and top with 5 raspberries. Place another disc of cake on top and dust the surface with icing (confectioners') sugar. Repeat the process so that you have 8 towers of loveliness.

Cherry buns

This was often made in the 1970s without the aid of a mixer. Just me, my wooden spoon and quite a lot of mess. I was utterly, utterly happy and all my thoughts about the lack of a Sindy pony in my life were forgotten because I was making cherry buns. I added the icing because, in my grown-up world, I can. In the 1970s, they were naked, but this is the exact recipe I used.

✳ Makes about 12

75 g/2 ½ oz/¼ cup plus
   1 tbsp margarine

75 g/2 ½ oz/⅓ cup caster
   (superfine) sugar

1 large free-range egg

125 g/4 ½ oz/½ cup plus
   1 tbsp flour, plain
   (all-purpose) or self-raising

1 tsp baking powder (omit if you
   are using self-raising flour)

grated zest of 1 unwaxed lemon

50 g/1 ¾ oz/2 tbsp glacé
   (candied) cherries, quartered

2–3 tbsp milk

Preheat the oven to 180°C/350°F/Gas mark 4. Line a 12-hole bun tin (pan) with paper cases (baking cups). Cream the margarine and sugar, using a wooden spoon (it said so, so I did), until the mixture is light and creamy. Beat in the egg.

Sift the flour and baking powder, if using, into a second bowl. Add the lemon zest and cherries to the flour and mix in. Add the flour to the creamed mixture and stir well so that all the ingredients are thoroughly mixed. Add enough milk to make the mixture just soft enough to drop from the spoon. Put a big teaspoonful into each paper case and bake for 20–25 minutes.

Maids of honour

Now, these little cakes were created in the 16th century at Richmond Palace. I tell you this because these ancient recipes seem to have hundreds of slightly different versions, all claiming to be the real one. I have no idea how you tell, so I have decided to be bold and go my own way. Some recipes use puff pastry, some use shortcrust. Some have currants, some have jam. I am going with lemon curd, because I like it, and a sweet pastry, because it doesn't go all tough and chewy. So, maybe these should be called Maids of Dishonour, because I have flagrantly mucked about with history. Sorry.

✳ Makes about 16

For the pastry:

175 g/6 oz/¾ cup unsalted butter

60 g/2 oz/scant ⅓ cup caster (superfine) sugar

pinch of salt

250 g/9 oz/2 ½ cups plain (all-purpose) flour

1 large free-range egg yolk

For the filling:

225 g/8 oz/1 cup curd cheese

45 g/1 ½ oz/scant ¼ cup caster (superfine) sugar

grated zest of 1 unwaxed lemon

25 g/1 oz/¼ cup ground almonds

1 large free-range egg

1 large free-range egg yolk

2 tbsp lemon curd

Make the pastry by beating the butter, sugar and salt together until really pale and fluffy. Add a spoonful of the flour and beat this in, followed by the egg yolk. Then beat in the remaining flour, a spoonful at a time. Finally, add just enough very cold water to bring the dough together. Turn it out onto a floured surface and give it a quick knead before wrapping it in cling film (plastic wrap) and chilling for at least 2 hours.

Preheat the oven to 180°C/350°F/Gas mark 4 and grease 16 tart tins (pans). Roll out the pastry to a thickness of 3 mm/⅛ in, cut out 16 circles using an 8 cm/3 ¼ in cutter and place the discs in the tins.

In a bowl, mix together the curd cheese, sugar, lemon zest, almonds, egg and egg yolk. Make sure that everything is really evenly mixed and amalgamated. Put a little lemon curd in the bottom of each pastry case and then fill each tart two-thirds full with the cheese mixture. Bake for about 25 minutes until puffy and golden. When you take them out, please don't despair when they sink down. This is what they do. Nothing you can do about it. Remember, only you saw them in the oven puffed up − no one else knows.

Date and candied
walnut scones

Date and walnut? Yes, please. Quick scones? Yes, please. Hurrah, a marriage made in heaven. There is a Devonian way of eating scones called Thunder and Lightning where, instead of the obligatory strawberry jam and clotted cream, you have black treacle and clotted cream. A revelation. It is just sensational with these scones.

✳ Makes about 10

25 g/1 oz/1 ¾ tbsp unsalted butter

100 g/3 ½ oz/¾ cup walnuts, chopped

2 tbsp caster (superfine) sugar

225 g/8 oz/2 cups self-raising flour

½ tsp salt

1 tsp baking powder

50 g/1 ¾ oz/scant ¼ cup unsalted butter

2 tsp caster (superfine) sugar

75 g/2 ½ oz/½ cup chopped dates

150 ml/5 fl oz/⅔ cup milk

1 large free-range egg white

clotted cream and black treacle, to serve

Preheat the oven to 220°C/425°F/Gas mark 7. In a frying pan, gently melt the butter. When it is frothy, tip in the walnuts and the caster (superfine) sugar and mix for a few minutes until all the nuts are well coated with buttery sugar. Tip the nuts onto a plate to cool. (If you wish, you can do this a day in advance and keep them in a an airtight container.)

Sift the flour, salt and baking powder into a large bowl. Rub in the butter until you have a mixture resembling fine breadcrumbs. Stir in the sugar and dates and enough milk to make a soft dough – you may not want to add all the milk all in one go.

Turn out the dough onto a floured surface and give it a quick knead. Roll it out until it is about 2.5 cm/1 in thick, and cut out the scones with a 5 cm/2 in cutter. Place the scones on a baking tray, brush them with the egg white and sprinkle the walnuts over the top. Bake for about 10 minutes until brown and well risen. Cool on a wire rack for 10 minutes or so and then split them, slather with clotted cream and trickle with treacle.

Eccles cakes

I love the thought of Eccles cakes, but whenever I eat them I realize why I don't have them more often: chopped mixed peel. Bleuch. I can't stand the stuff. It makes me shudder just to think about it, sitting there all orange and yellow in its little round tub, just waiting to make you contort your face in disgust. I made Eccles cakes with just currants. They were lovely. Someone should make it the law. Much nicer.

✻ Makes about 10

1 x 500 g/18 oz packet all-butter puff pastry

25 g/1 oz/1 ¾ tbsp very soft unsalted butter

75 g/2 ½ oz/½ cup currants

25 g/1 oz/2 tbsp dark muscovado sugar

finely grated zest of 1 unwaxed lemon

finely grated zest of 1 orange

1–2 drops of lemon oil (optional)

caster (superfine) sugar for sprinkling

Preheat the oven to 220°C/425°F/Gas mark 7. Roll out the pastry to about 3 mm/⅛ in thick and cut out 10 rounds (more if you can). In a bowl, mix the butter, currants, sugar and fruit zests. I sometimes add a drop or two of lemon oil to the proceedings.

Place a teaspoon of the mixture into the very centre of each pastry circle. Bundle up the outer edges as if to make a purse and squidge the edges together to seal the little parcel. Turn each one over, seal-side down, and roll it out into a flatter circle so that the currants just start to peek through. Prick all over with a fork and place on the baking tray. Repeat the process until they are all done and then bake for about 15 minutes or until golden brown. When they are out of the oven, transfer to a wire rack and sprinkle with caster (superfine) sugar while they are still warm.

Ginger and lemon morsels

These are a cross between a biscuit and a cake, but as they are made in cake cases and are particularly delicious, I reckon they deserve to be here.

✳ Makes 12

225 g/8 oz/1 cup unsalted butter

75 g/2 ½ oz/½ cup icing (confectioners') sugar

200 g/7 oz/scant 2 cups plain (all-purpose) flour

25 g/1 oz/2 ½ tbsp cornflour (cornstarch)

3 tsp ground ginger

2 tbsp milk

2 tbsp lemon curd

2 tbsp icing (confectioners') sugar, sifted

juice of 1 lemon

Preheat the oven to 180°C/350°F/Gas mark 4 and line a 2-hole muffin tin (pan) with paper cases (baking cups). Beat the butter and icing (confectioners') sugar together until pale and fluffy, then beat in the flour, cornflour (cornstarch) and ginger. Beat in the milk – the mixture will still be very stiff.

Transfer teaspoons of the mixture to the paper cases and level it out with the back of a teaspoon – you need to be quite firm. Then take the handle of a wooden spoon and mush a hole in the centre of each cake. Bake in the oven for about 20 minutes or until golden. When you take them out of the oven, get that wooden spoon back and mush those holes again. You have to do this as soon as they are out of the oven because, as they cool, they crisp up.

Leave the cakes to cool in the tin. When they are cold, put a little blob of lemon curd into each hole. Make a thin icing with the icing sugar and lemon juice and drizzle it over the top of the cakes. Wait for an hour or so for the icing to dry before tucking in.

Teacakes

This is my version of the tea-time classic. We used to have them as special treats at birthday parties and, to be honest, I find them just as delicious now as I did when I was seven. My teacakes, though I say so myself, are yummy and a doddle to make. The biscuit recipe makes far more biscuits than you probably want teacakes (48 to be precise). I have worked on the idea of making 15 teacakes and using the rest of the dough to make plain biscuits – or it can be frozen.

✳ Makes 15

250 g/9 oz/1 cup plus 1 tbsp unsalted butter, softened

140 g/4 ¾ oz /1 cup icing (confectioners') sugar, sifted

1 tsp vanilla extract

1 large free-range egg yolk

375 g/13 oz/3 ¾ cups plain (all-purpose) flour

approx 2 tbsp raspberry or strawberry jam

15 marshmallows

200 g/7 oz milk chocolate

First, make the biscuit dough by beating the butter and sugar together until creamy. Add the vanilla and the egg yolk and continue beating for a few moments, then tip in the flour and work it all together into a smooth dough. Tip it out onto a floured surface and knead it for a few moments, then wrap it in cling film (plastic wrap) and chill it in the fridge for a couple of hours.

After the allotted chilling time, preheat the oven to 180°C/350°F/Gas mark 4 and line a couple of baking sheets with silicone liners. Roll out the dough to about 5 mm/¼ in thick and cut out 15 rounds with a 4 cm/1 ½ in cutter. Place the biscuits on the sheets and bake for about 10 minutes, or until they are golden brown. Leave the biscuits on the baking sheet for a couple of minutes before carefully placing them on wire racks to cool and firm up.

When the biscuits are cold, spread a little bit of jam over each one and place a marshmallow on top. Break up the chocolate and put it in a heatproof bowl over a pan of barely simmering water – don't let the water touch the bottom of the bowl. Melt the chocolate slowly. When it is lovely and runny, drizzle the chocolate over the marshmallow and let it run down the sides and over the biscuit so that the whole of the top of the teacake is smothered in chocolate. This is much less hazardous if you leave the teacakes on the wire rack and place the whole thing over a tray to catch the drips. Let the chocolate harden and set. If the teacakes are a bit stuck to the rack, use a warm palette knife to coax them off.

Tea breads, buns and loaves

Afternoon tea is my all-time favourite meal. I love the selection of little bits and bobs – a slice of this and a slither of that. No proper tea is complete without some form of bread. It might be a yeastless tea bread – often a fruity loaf which matures over a day or two and then demands a thick slab of butter to out-do any goodness from the generally low-fat and low-sugar recipe. These are cakes that can be made in the blink of an eye and bunged in the oven. They require no skill, are extremely well-behaved and positively welcome a spell in the deep freeze, to be plucked out at a later date.

A yeast-based bun or loaf calls for a bit more planning, but the results are always spectacularly impressive. They might require a bit of commitment in the time department, but they really don't need great levels of baking skill. I was always a bit terrified of recipes that involved yeast. I have no idea why. It's magical, lovely stuff. Kneading dough is a really pleasurable experience, and the moment when the dough changes from rather stringy and snaggly to silken and smooth never fails to amaze me. But, believe me, a loaf or bun made at home with yeast needs to be eaten that day. If it looks like it's not all going down the hatch, freeze it.

Dried yeast is readily available all over the place. Fresh yeast is not generally for sale, but if you ask your local baker they will generally provide you with some. I have also asked at the bakery department in several supermarkets and they have never let me down.

Little loaf cases are also widely available these days, so do experiment with making smaller versions of any of these loaves – just remember to alter the timings as they won't need as long in the oven.

Gently spiced fruit loaf

This is the sort of fruity bread that makes people whimper slightly. It has everything: warm spices, gorgeous fruit, soft bread and a drizzle of lemony icing. Ooooh. Yes, please. You decide what fruit to use – it's all good.

✳ Makes a large loaf that will serve 8 peckish people

For the dough:

40 g/1 ½ oz/2 ¾ tbsp unsalted butter

275 g/9 ½ oz/2 cups strong white bread flour

50 g/1 ¾ oz/scant ¼ cup caster (superfine) sugar

pinch of salt

7 g/¼ oz sachet dried yeast

100 ml/3 ½ fl oz/scant ½ cup hand-hot milk

3 large free-range egg yolks

For the filling:

500 ml/17 fl oz/scant 2 cups water

450 g/1 lb/2 cups dried fruit (apricots, cranberries, dates, figs, peaches, etc.), chopped

zest and juice of 1 large unwaxed lemon

zest and juice of 1 large orange

2 tbsp runny honey

1 tsp ground coriander

1 tsp cardamom seeds, crushed

For the icing:

75 g/2 ½ oz/½ cup icing (confectioners') sugar, sifted

juice of 1 large lemon

flaked almonds, to sprinkle (optional)

Start by making the dough. In a large bowl, rub the butter into the flour until it resembles breadcrumbs and then stir in the sugar, salt and yeast. Pour in the hot milk and 2 egg yolks and mix to form a dough. Turn the dough out onto a floured surface and knead the dough until it's smooth and elastic – this will take at least 10 minutes. Put the dough back into the bowl and cover with a tea towel or a layer of cling film (plastic wrap) and leave to prove somewhere warm for at least 1 hour. The dough should double in size.

While the dough is proving, crack on with the filling. Put the water in a big saucepan and bring it to the boil. Add the chopped dried fruit and simmer, stirring every now and again until the fruit is really soft. Add the citrus zest and juice, honey and spices and continue bubbling gently until the liquid has been absorbed by the fruit. Stir it every so often as it can catch on the bottom of the pan if left alone too long. Leave the mixture to cool down.

When the dough has doubled in size and the fruity filling is cool, take the dough out of the bowl and give it 2–3 bashes to knock the air out of it. Knead it again for another 3–4 minutes, then roll it out into a large rectangle about 1 cm/½ in thick. Spread the fruit over the surface, leaving a gap around the edge of about 2 cm/¾ in. Roll up the dough as you would a Swiss roll (jelly roll) and press the edges together to seal, then coil it round so you end up with a circular sausage. Place it on a baking tray with the seal underneath. Pop the tea towel over the top again and leave it in the warm place for another hour to prove.

Preheat the oven to 180°C/350°F/Gas mark 4 and, just before the loaf goes in the oven, brush it all over with the remaining egg yolk. Bake for about 20 minutes. It will be done when it is risen and golden on the top and the bottom sounds hollow when you give it a knock. Cool the loaf on a wire rack and make a very thin icing with the icing (confectioners') sugar and lemon juice. When cool, randomly drizzle the icing over the top of the loaf.

Chelsea buns

Hands up, who doesn't love a Chelsea bun? They may not be the most elegant, but not many people will turn one down and you get many, many Brownie points for making them yourself.

✴ Makes 12

225 g/8 oz/1 ½ cups strong white bread flour, plus extra for dusting

½ tsp salt

60 g/2 oz/¼ cup unsalted butter

1 ½ tsp dried yeast

100 ml/3 ½ fl oz/scant ½ cup hand-hot milk

1 large free-range egg, beaten

50 g/1 ¾ oz/⅓ cup currants

50 g/1 ¾ oz/⅓ cup raisins

2 tsp cinnamon

75 g/2 ½ oz/about ½ cup dark muscovado sugar

2 tbsp icing (confectioners') sugar, sifted

2 tbsp granulated sugar

Put the flour and salt into a big bowl and rub in 40 g/1 ½ oz/ 2 ¾ tbsp butter until the mixture looks like breadcrumbs. Then stir in the yeast. Pour the milk into the flour mixture along with the egg. Give everything a good old mix until it forms a dough.

Flour your work surface and knead the dough for at least 10 minutes until it becomes silky and smooth and really elastic. Pop it back in the bowl, cover with cling film (plastic wrap) and put the bowl in a warm place for about 1 hour, or until the dough has doubled in size.

Remove the dough from the bowl and give it a quick bash and a knead, then roll it out into a rectangle measuring about 30 x 25 cm/12 x 10 in. Melt the remaining butter. In another bowl, mix together the dried fruit, cinnamon and brown sugar. Brush the rectangle of dough with the melted butter and then sprinkle the sugary fruit mixture evenly over, leaving a border of about 2 cm/¾ in around the edges. Roll up the dough as if you were making a Swiss roll (jelly roll) and then cut the roll into 12 slices. Place them on a baking sheet (I line mine with silicone paper, but you could grease and flour yours if you prefer) with plenty of room in between each bun. Cover again with cling film and leave for another hour in a warm place to prove.

Preheat the oven to 180°C/350°F/Gas mark 4. When you return to the buns they should have puffed up and started nestling up to one another. Bake for about 20 minutes or until risen, golden and desirable. Take them out of the oven and make a thin glaze with the icing (confectioners') sugar and enough water to give you a consistency like milk. Brush the glaze over the buns and sprinkle with granulated sugar.

Fougasses

We're going all French again with this one. Those French really know their way around a bread product. Fougasse is generally a sweet bread which comes in many different sizes, but essentially the effect is the same. You tear bits off and dunk them into milky coffee and sigh with pleasure. If you want a savoury version, reduce the sugar and the sweet flavourings and stud the top with olives and anchovies. Please note that this dough takes longer to prove than some other breads – don't be tempted to reduce the proving time as the results won't be as good.

✳ Makes 8 small fougasses
225 g/8 oz/1 ½ cups strong white bread flour
80 g/2 ¾ oz/⅓ cup caster (superfine) sugar
½ tsp salt
grated zest of 1 orange
1 tsp dried yeast
75 ml/2 ½ fl oz/scant ⅓ cup warm water
2 tbsp olive oil
1 large free-range egg, beaten
½ tsp orange flower water
milk, to glaze
1 tsp fennel seeds

Mix together the flour, sugar, salt, orange zest and yeast. Add the warm water, olive oil, egg and orange flower water and mix everything together until it forms a dough. Tip the mixture onto a floured surface and knead for about 10 minutes or until the dough becomes soft, smooth and elastic. Put the dough back in the bowl, cover with cling film (plastic wrap) and place the bowl somewhere warm for at least 2 hours or until the dough has doubled in size.

Knead the dough again and then cut it into 8 equal-sized pieces. Roll each piece into an oval about 5 mm/¼ in thick and then, with a pair of scissors, cut about 6 slashes all the way through the dough. When you give the dough a bit of a tug, the slashes should open out a bit more. Transfer each fougasse to a lined baking tray, cover and prove the dough again for about 30 minutes.

Preheat the oven to 200°C/400°F/Gas mark 6. Brush the fougasses with milk and sprinkle the fennel seeds over the top – you may need to push them in slightly to get them to stick. Bake the fougasses for 15–20 minutes or until they are golden brown.

Marmalade and apricot tea bread (for Dad)

When in need of a snack to keep him going, my Dad used to wander round the house clutching a marmalade sandwich. This tea bread is dedicated to him. If he were still here, he'd probably enjoy it, but I do acknowledge that he'd secretly be hankering after the white bread and thick-cut Chivers approach.

✱ Makes 10 slices

200 g/7 oz/scant 2 cups plain (all-purpose) flour

2 tsp ground ginger

1 tsp baking powder

50 g/1 ¾ oz/scant ¼ cup unsalted butter

50 g/1 ¾ oz/¼ cup light muscovado sugar

4 tbsp marmalade

75 ml/2 ½ fl oz/scant ⅓ cup milk

1 large free-range egg, beaten

100 g/3 ½ oz/scant ⅔ cup ready-to-eat dried apricots, chopped

Preheat the oven to 160°C/325°F/Gas mark 3. Grease and line a 450 g/1 lb loaf tin (pan). Sift the flour, ginger and baking powder into a large bowl and rub in the butter until the mixture looks like breadcrumbs. Then stir in the sugar and the chopped apricots. In another bowl, or a jug, mix up the marmalade, milk and egg and pour that onto the dry mixture. Mix it all up really well and pour it into the tin. Level the top and bake for about 1 hour, or until golden, firm to the touch and a skewer comes out cleanly. Turn the loaf onto a wire rack to cool.

I sometimes make some candied orange peel to go on top, but this is entirely optional. If you want to, all you need to do is carefully pare some strips of orange peel and put them into a pan with about 150 ml/5 fl oz/⅔ cup water and 3 tbsp caster (superfine) sugar. Bring the pan to the boil and then slowly simmer for about an hour or until the peel has gone translucent and the liquid has reduced by about half. Don't let the liquid reduce to a caramel or you will end up with something else altogether! Remove the orange strips from the pan and leave on silicone paper to cool and dry. Sprinkle with more caster sugar if you wish.

Apple and walnut tea bread

This tea bread has to be one of the most versatile numbers going. Make it sweet, make it savoury, make it big, make it small – it really is a wonder. Just delicious with a lump of strong Cheddar, or equally good with a smear of butter and a cup of tea – even au naturel, shoved in a lunch box. It's easy to make and keeps well for ages in a tin. Surely this recipe must belong to a 'hero' category?

✳ Makes 1 big loaf or
   12 small ones

100 g/3 ½ oz/scant ½ cup
   unsalted butter

100 g/3 ½ oz/scant ½ cup caster
   (superfine) sugar

2 large free-range eggs

1 tbsp golden syrup

100 g/3 ½ oz/⅔ cup sultanas
   (golden raisins)

100 g/3 ½ oz/¾ cup
   chopped walnuts

225 g/8 oz/2 cups
   self-raising flour

1 tsp mixed spice

1 tsp ground cinnamon

2 dessert apples, peeled,
   cored and chopped
   (I use Braeburn or Cox's)

Preheat the oven to 160°C/325°F/Gas mark 3. Grease and line a 680 g/1½ lb loaf tin (pan) or lay out 12 mini loaf cases on a baking tray. Put all the ingredients into a big bowl and give them a bit of a beating. I bung them in the mixer because I'm lazy, but a wooden spoon would be just as good. Don't use a food processor, though, because you will pulverize the apple too much.

Tip the lot onto the tin and bake the biggie for about 1 hour or the littlies for about 20 minutes. A knife or skewer will come out cleanly when they are cooked. Cool the big one on a wire rack and leave the little ones to cool in their cases.

Fig and raisin tea bread

I don't think we generally cook enough with dried figs. I adore them and encourage you to use them at every opportunity. Naturally sweet, soft, yet slightly crunchy from the seeds and really, really good for you. Yum.

✱ Makes 10 slices

225 g/8 oz/2 cups plain (all-purpose) flour

100 g/3 ½ oz/scant ½ cup unsalted butter

100 g/3 ½ oz/⅔ cup dried figs, chopped

100 g/3 ½ oz/½ cup demerara sugar

50 g/1 ¾ oz/scant ½ cup chopped pecan nuts (optional)

100 g/3 ½ oz/⅔ cup raisins

1 tsp baking powder

1 tsp bicarbonate of soda (baking soda)

150 ml/5 fl oz/⅔ cup milk

Preheat the oven to 160°C/325°F/Gas mark 3. Grease and line a 1 kg/2 lb loaf tin (pan). Put the flour into a large bowl and rub the butter into it until the mixture looks like breadcrumbs. Stir in the figs, sugar, pecan nuts (if you are using them) and raisins.

Mix the baking powder, bicarbonate of soda (baking soda) and milk together and pour into the dry mix. Mix really well, adding a drop more milk if you need to, so that you have a good dropping consistency. Tip the mixture into the tin and bake for about 1 hour or until firm to the touch and a knife or skewer comes out cleanly. Cool the loaf on a wire rack.

Date and walnut tea bread

Dates appear often in this chapter, probably because they have a natural affinity with tea breads. Their sweetness and moistness adds not just flavour but the gorgeous texture that is called for here. Dates and walnuts, of course, are no strangers and so it is only right and proper that they appear together in a tea bread.

✳ Makes about 12 slices

110 g/4 oz/½ cup
  unsalted butter

3 tbsp golden syrup

1 tbsp black treacle

150 ml/5 fl oz/⅔ cup milk

2 large free-range eggs

225 g/8 oz/1 ¾ cups wholemeal
  plain (all-purpose) flour

1 tsp cinnamon

1 tsp bicarbonate of soda
  (baking soda)

100 g/3 ½ oz/¾ cup
  chopped walnuts

150 g/5 oz/1 ¼ cups stoned
  dates, chopped

Preheat the oven to 160°C/325°F/Gas mark 3. Grease and line a 1 kg/2 lb loaf tin (pan). Melt the butter, syrup and treacle together in a pan over a low heat until well amalgamated and then, off the heat, stir in the milk. Let the mixture cool a little more and then beat in the eggs (if you add them too soon you will end up with scrambled eggs).

Sift the dry ingredients into a large bowl (I use the freestanding mixer) and then beat in the syrup mixture. Fold in the walnuts and dates, tip the mixture into the tin and bake for about 1 ½ hours. It is done when a knife or skewer comes out clean. Cool in the tin.

Fruity fruit tea tea bread

I know one shouldn't have favourites when writing recipes – it's a bit like having a favourite child. Feels a bit wrong. But, whisper it, this is my favourite tea bread – and it's fat-free, which makes slathering on a thick slab of butter seem like a pretty sensible idea. It's moist, packed with plump, juicy fruit, sweet enough to satisfy pangs for something sugary and keeps you going. Although it's scrumptious with butter, it's also perfectly delicious naked. Experiment with both the fruit and the type of tea – I can almost guarantee deliciousness. Cranberry and sanguinello orange are favourites with me at the moment.

✳ Serves 10

300 ml/10 fl oz/1 ¼ cups strong fruit tea

100 g/3 ½ oz/⅔ cup raisins

100 g/3 ½ oz/scant ⅔ cup ready-to-eat dried apricots, chopped

100 g/3 ½ oz/⅔ cup dried figs, chopped

1 large free-range egg

75 g/2 ½ oz/generous ½ cup wholemeal plain (all-purpose) flour

75 g/2 ½ oz/scant ¾ cup plain (all-purpose) flour

50 g/1 ¾ oz/¼ cup light muscovado sugar

1 tsp baking powder

2 tbsp milk

Put the tea and the dried fruit in a saucepan and bring to the boil. Simmer gently for 30 minutes, but don't let the tea evaporate completely. Leave to cool for 10 minutes or so.

Preheat the oven to 160°C/325°F/Gas mark 3. Grease and line a 680 g/1 ½ lb loaf tin (pan). Tip the fruit and tea into a big bowl and simply add all the other ingredients. Mix really well so that everything is incorporated, tip the mixture into the loaf tin and level the surface. Bake for about 1 hour or until it is firm to the touch and a knife or skewer comes out clean.

Cool on a wire rack before cutting into thick slices and eating with your eyes shut (it's that sort of tea bread).

Sticky date tea bread

I need to come clean – I've adapted this from a Delia Smith recipe. Delia's original will always be Delia's and it's very good. I wouldn't dare to say that mine is better. Oh no. Just different. (It is a good tea bread, though.)

✱ Makes about 12 slices

325 g/11 oz/scant 2 ¼ cups stoned dates, chopped

325 g/11 oz/scant 2 ¼ cups raisins

275 g/9 ½ oz/1 ¼ cups unsalted butter

275 ml/9 fl oz/1 cup plus 2 tbsp water

397 g/14 oz can condensed milk

150 g/5 oz/1 ⅓ cups plain (all-purpose) flour

150 g/5 oz/scant 1 ¼ cups wholemeal flour

1 tsp bicarbonate of soda (baking soda)

1 tbsp ginger marmalade

Preheat the oven to 170°C/325°F/Gas mark 3. Grease and line a 1 kg/2 lb loaf tin (pan) – I use a ready-made loaf liner for this one. Put the dates and raisins in a pan with the butter, water and condensed milk. Bring to the boil, stirring all the time to stop it sticking, and then simmer the mixture for 3 minutes, continuing to stir. Take the pan off the heat, tip the mixture into a bowl and leave to cool.

When the mixture has cooled, add the flour, bicarbonate of soda (baking soda) and marmalade and give it all a vigorous stir. Tip it into the loaf tin, level the surface and bake for about 45 minutes – it may need a little longer. You will need to keep an eye on the top of the cake. If it looks as if it is over-browning, cover it with greaseproof paper (parchment paper). The cake is done when a knife or skewer comes out clean. Cool it in the tin. You can then store it for weeks in an airtight tin should you wish to.

Earl Grey loaf

If you don't like Earl Grey tea you could use another type – try Assam, Darjeeling or Lapsang Souchong. If push comes to shove, use builder's tea. And no, I haven't made a mistake – there isn't any fat in this one either. Hurrah for that. Again, you can butter it at will.

✳ Serves 10

25 g/8 oz/1 ½ cups raisins or sultanas (golden raisins)

175 ml/6 fl oz/¾ cup strong cold Earl Grey tea

225 g/8 oz/2 cups self-raising flour

175 g/6 oz/¾ cup demerara sugar

1 large free-range egg

Soak the raisins in the tea overnight. The next day, preheat the oven to 160°C/325°F/Gas mark 3 and grease and line a 680 g/1 ½ lb loaf tin (pan). If you haven't been organized enough to soak your fruit, don't panic – put the raisins and the tea in a saucepan, bring to the boil and simmer gently for 20 minutes. Not quite as good, but not bad.

Tip the fruit and remaining tea into a large bowl and simply stir in everything else. That's it. Tip the mixture into the tin and bake for about 1 hour or until a knife or skewer comes out cleanly. Let the cake cool in the tin for 10 minutes before turning out onto a wire rack.

Malt loaf

I remember that after number one son was born the midwife told me that malt loaf was an ideal snack for breastfeeding women – full of energy-giving properties, packed with vitamins, easy to eat one-handed and really a bit of a superfood. I took her advice very seriously and consumed absolutely gargantuan quantities of the stuff. It was just the excuse I was looking for. It was quite a while before I could face any again. However, those days are long gone and I happily tuck in to malt loaf with the same gusto as all those years ago. Malt extract is available in health food shops.

✳ Makes about 8 slices

110 g/4 oz/¾ cup raisins

110 g/4 oz/¾ cup sultanas (golden raisins)

40 g/1 ½ oz/2 ¾ tbsp unsalted butter

150 ml/5 fl oz/⅔ cup water

175 g/6 oz/1 ½ cups self-raising flour

½ tsp bicarbonate of soda (baking soda)

pinch of salt

110 g/4 oz/⅔ cup dark muscovado sugar

1 large free-range egg, beaten

1 tbsp malt extract

Preheat the oven to 180°C/350°F/Gas mark 4. Grease and line a 500 g/1 lb 2 oz loaf tin (pan). Put the dried fruit, butter and water into a saucepan, bring to the boil and then simmer gently for 5 minutes. Let the mixture cool for a bit.

In a large bowl, mix together the flour, bicarbonate of soda (baking soda), salt and sugar. Stir in the wet mixture followed by the egg and the malt. Give everything a jolly good stir. Tip the mixture into the tin and bake for about 1 hour or until a knife or skewer comes out clean. Cool in the tin, then slice, butter and tuck in.

Cheesy twirl buns

Make these and there will be an unseemly dash for the plate to get hold of them. They're delicious warm or cold, but eat them on the day you bake them. You can happily freeze the little cherubs in their uncooked state and pop them in the oven straight from the freezer.

✳ Makes about 10

250 g/9 oz/1 cup low-fat cream cheese such as Quark

100 g/3 ½ oz/¾ cup finely grated Cheddar cheese

100 g/3 ½ oz/½ cup finely grated parmesan cheese

2 tsp English mustard powder

500 g/1 lb 2 oz packet all-butter puff pastry

1 large free-range egg yolk

Preheat the oven to 180°C/350°F/Gas mark 4. In a bowl, mix together the cream cheese, the grated cheeses and the mustard powder until you have a smoothish paste.

On a floured surface, roll out the pastry to a rectangle about 2 mm/⅛ in thick. Spread the mixture over half the pastry, leaving a border of about 2 cm/¾ in around the edge, and fold the uncovered half over the cheesy half. Roll this a couple of times to thin it out and squidge the filling a bit, then fold the pastry in half and roll again a few times. Fold the pastry once more and then roll until you have a rectangle about 5 mm/¼ in thick. Cut into strips about 2 cm/¾ in wide.

Put a sheet of silicone paper or liner on a baking sheet. Take a strip of pastry and twist it as if you were making a cheese straw. Coil the twisted strip up into a saucer shape, tuck the end underneath and place on the baking sheet. Repeat with all the strips. Brush the top of all the pastries with the beaten egg yolk and bake for about 15 minutes or until puffed up and golden with cheesy ooze peering out here and there.

Cheddar and rosemary bread

This lovely loaf can be made freeform to have hunks torn off for lunch or baked in a loaf tin for thin slices, buttered and quartered and presented nicely on a plate for afternoon tea. For a right old English tea-time malarkey, spread it with a thin layer of Gentleman's Relish – now we're talking. The herb doesn't have to be rosemary – thyme would also be great – and the cheese doesn't have to be Cheddar. Any hard cheese with plenty of flavour would be fine.

✳ Makes a 2 lb loaf

500 g/1 lb 2 oz/3 ¼ cups strong white bread flour, plus extra for dusting

1 tsp salt

1 tsp caster (superfine) sugar

3 tsp English mustard powder

10 g/⅓ oz dried yeast

300 ml/10 fl oz/1 ¼ cups tepid water

2 tsp fresh rosemary, chopped

300 g/10 oz/10 ½ cups grated strong Cheddar cheese

In a large bowl, stir together the flour, salt, sugar, mustard powder and yeast, then add the water and mix until a dough forms. Tip the dough onto a well-floured work surface and get kneading like you mean it for at least 10 minutes, but maybe 15. You may stop when the dough is smooth and elastic and doesn't feel straggly under your fingers. Form the dough into a ball and score a large, deep cross in the top. Put it back in the bowl, cover with a tea towel and leave somewhere warm to prove – this will probably take about 1 hour.

When the dough has doubled in size, bash it about to knock out all the air and start kneading again, this time adding 200 g/7 oz/1 ⅔ cups grated cheese in three goes. Just sprinkle a third over the dough and start kneading; when it has been incorporated, add the next third and so on. When all the cheese is in, knead the dough for another 5 minutes before either forming it into a loose shape and placing on a baking tray, or putting it into a greased and floured 1 kg/2 lb tin (pan). Make lots of dimpled holes in the top of the loaf with your fingers, sprinkle the mustard powder and remaining cheese over the top and prod in a bit more. Cover the dough again with the tea towel and leave once more in the warm place to prove for another hour.

Preheat the oven to 190°C/375°F/Gas mark 5. The baking time depends on what shape you have made, but it should be around the 20-minute mark. You will know when it is done by tapping the bottom of the loaf. If it sounds hollow, it is ready. If you have cooked it in a tin, turn out onto a wire rack to cool.

The snuggle loaf

Why is this chocolatey, hazelnutty, soft, sweet hunk of loveliness called 'the snuggle loaf', I hear you cry? Because, dear hearts, eating it is like being enveloped in the warmest, most comforting hug you have ever had. A right, proper snuggle.

✳ Serves 4–8

200 g/7 oz/2 cups strong white bread flour

45 g/1 ½ oz/scant ¼ cup caster (superfine) sugar

pinch of salt

25 g/1 oz/1 ¾ tbsp unsalted butter

7 g/¼ oz dried yeast

5 tbsp hand-hot milk

1 large free-range egg, beaten

2 tsp Nutella, or other chocolate spread

2 tbsp hazelnuts, roasted, skinned and chopped

50 g/1 ¾ oz dark (bittersweet) chocolate, chopped into small chunks

2 tbsp icing (confectioners') sugar

First, make the base dough by putting the flour and sugar into a large bowl followed by a pinch of salt. Rub the butter into this mixture until it resembles breadcrumbs and then stir in the yeast. Tip in the milk, followed by the egg, and mix everything up until you get a dough. Turn it onto a floured surface and knead for at least 10 minutes or until the dough is beautifully smooth, silky and elastic. Pop the dough back in the bowl, cover it with a tea towel and put it somewhere warm to prove for 1 hour, or until it has doubled in size.

Knead the dough again for another 5 minutes and then split it into halves. Roll both lumps into strips about 25 x 10 cm/10 x 4 in. Spread a spoonful of Nutella down the middle of each strip, followed by a sprinkling of the nuts and the chocolate. Keep back about half a tablespoonful of the nuts for sprinkling on the top of the loaf. Roll up each rectangle as you would a Swiss roll (jelly roll). Take each sausage and twist them round one another so you have a twisty loaf. I then like to shove both ends towards each other to shorten it and fatten it up a bit. Pop the loaf on a greased and floured baking tray and cover again with the tea towel. Leave it to prove and consider its fate for another hour.

Preheat the oven to 160°C/325°F/Gas mark 3 and, when the loaf is ready, bake it for 20–25 minutes until golden brown, risen and totally glorious. While it's cooling, mix enough water with the icing (confectioners') sugar to create a thin glaze the consistency of single (light) cream and brush it all over the top of the loaf. Sprinkle the remaining hazelnuts over while the glaze is still wet.

Prepare your surroundings for your snuggle experience. Sofa, duvet, hot-water bottle, tea, Richard Curtis film all pretty standard.

Cranberry and apricot panettone

Do you want to make friends and influence people? Do you have a spare couple of hours? Make panettone! Another classic recipe for jiggling flavours. Try different fruits, chunks of chocolate, nuts, honey glazes, sugars ... Make them big or small – oh yes, they really are the business. Panettone cases can be found in some kitchen shops and online emporia.

✳ Makes 8 small or 1 large panettone

2 vanilla pods

2 large free-range eggs

5 egg yolks (save 1 egg white for glazing)

250 g/9 oz/1 cup plus 2 tbsp unsalted butter, softened

100 g/3 ½ oz/scant ½ cup caster (superfine) sugar, plus 1 tsp

grated zest of 2 unwaxed lemons

75 ml/2 ½ fl oz/scant ⅓ cup milk

25 g/1 oz fresh yeast, or 20 g/ ⅔ oz dried yeast

500 g/1 lb 2 oz/3 ¼ cups strong white bread flour

1 tsp salt

175 g/6 oz/scant 1 ¼ cup craisins (dried cranberries)

100 g/3 ½ oz/scant ⅔ cup ready-to-eat dried apricots, chopped

Using greaseproof (parchment) paper, double line a 20 cm/ 8 in loose-bottomed cake tin. Extend the paper about 10 cm/ 4 in above the tin. Split the vanilla pods along their lengths and scrape out all the seeds. Put the whole eggs and the egg yolks in a bowl and add the vanilla seeds. Give it all a good old whisk up.

In a large bowl, beat the butter and sugar (except for 1 tsp) until pale and creamy and gradually add the egg and vanilla mixture. Add the lemon zest and beat away. Warm the milk to hand-hot and remove from the heat. Crumble in the fresh (or dried) yeast and a teaspoon of sugar and stir until the yeast dissolves. Set it aside and it will start to magically froth. Exciting.

Sift the flour into a large bowl and add the salt. Pour in the milky yeast and give it a stir, then add the buttery egg mixture and mix that in, too. Tip it all out onto a floured work surface and start bringing it all together. Now, this dough is initially super-sticky. Don't worry, it will sort itself out! Keep kneading for about 10 minutes until you get a silky-smooth dough. Pop it back in the bowl, cover with a tea towel or cling film (plastic wrap) and place somewhere warm for about 1 hour or until doubled in size.

Take the dough out of the bowl and knock the air out, then sprinkle the fruit over the dough and start kneading it all in until you get an even distribution. If making one panettone, shape it into a ball and bung it into the panettone case or cake tin (pan). If making mini ones, split the dough into 8 and place in the cases. Cover again and prove in a warm place for another 2 hours.

Preheat the oven to 180°C/350°F/Gas mark 4. Brush the top of the panettone with egg white. If you want to sprinkle anything on top, this is the time to do it. Then pop into the oven for 20 minutes for the littlies or 35–40 minutes for the whopper. It's done when a skewer comes out clean. Cool on a wire rack.

Brioche

Now, I think of brioche in the same category as panettone – not something that might spring into your mind as an obvious home-baked product. Give it a go. As with all these things, it's not actually as difficult as you might imagine, and the smells that waft through your house are positively dreamy. If you're going to do this properly, you need a 1.1 litre/ 2 pt fluted brioche mould – widely available in kitchen shops. Otherwise, do what I do and use whatever you have to hand – er – a loaf tin.

✳ Makes 1 large loaf or 8 small

15 g/½ oz fresh yeast, or 10 g/ ⅓ oz dried yeast

1 ½ tbsp warm water

50 g/1 ¾ oz/scant ¼ cup unsalted butter

225 g/8 oz/1 ½ cups strong white bread flour

1 tbsp caster (superfine) sugar

½ tsp salt

3 large free-range eggs, beaten

First, brush the mould or tin (pan) you are using with oil. Really take care here and get it into every nook and cranny – even if it's a non-stick pan, treat it like it isn't.

Crumble the fresh (or dried) yeast into the warm water and stir it around until it has dissolved. Set it to one side and let it do its magic and start frothing (this will take about 15 minutes).

Melt the butter and leave to cool slightly. Then put the flour, sugar, salt, melted butter, 2 eggs and yeasty liquid into a big bowl and mix it all together to make a dough. Tip the dough onto a floured work surface and knead for about 10–15 minutes until the dough is smooth, silky and beautifully elastic. Put the ball of dough back in the bowl, cover with cling film (plastic wrap) and leave to prove for about 1 hour. Scoring a deep cross in the top of the dough really helps with the proving.

After the dough has doubled in size, take it out of the bowl and give it another knead for 5 minutes. Then cut off two-thirds, form it into a ball and put it in the bottom of your mould. With your fingers, form a large hole in the centre of the ball and push right down to the bottom of the tin. Get your third of dough and form a ball that 'plugs' the hole – you'll have a knob sticking up. It is meant to look like this. Cover again with cling film and leave the brioche to prove again. It is done when the dough looks light and puffy and has almost reached the top of the tin.

Preheat the oven to 230°C/450°F/Gas mark 8 (yes, it is hot). Brush the top of the brioche with the remaining beaten egg and bake for about 15 minutes or until golden delicious. Try to let it cool slightly before tucking in. Manners.

Lardy cake

Right, let's get this out of the way: this is possibly the most unhealthy, artery-clogging cake you will ever come across. It is also part of Britain's heritage and has been around for years and years because it is so amazingly delicious. It is filling, sweet, doughy, chewy and comforting.

✳ Serves 8

25 g/1 oz fresh yeast, or 20 g/⅔ oz dried yeast

300 ml/10 fl oz/1 ¼ cups warm water

1 tsp caster (superfine) sugar

450 g/1 lb/4 ½ cups strong white bread flour

2 tsp salt

175 g/6 oz/¾ cup lard, chilled

80 g/2 ½ oz/½ cup currants

80 g/2 ½ oz/½ cup sultanas

80 g/2 ½ oz/½ cup raisins

175 g/6 oz/¾ cup caster (superfine) sugar

Grease a tin (pan) measuring about 20 x 25 cm/8 x 10 in. Crumble the fresh (or dried) yeast over the warm water and add the teaspoon of sugar. Blend it all so that the yeast dissolves, and set to one side for 15 minutes.

Pop the flour and salt into a large bowl and add just a tablespoon of the lard. Rub the lard into the flour and then add the yeast liquid. Mix it all up so that it forms a dough. Turn the dough out onto a floured surface and knead for about 10 minutes or until smooth and elastic. Put the dough back in the bowl, cover with cling film (plastic wrap) and leave somewhere warm for 30 minutes to prove. It doesn't need a proper prove like bread.

Take the dough out of the bowl, knock out the air and roll it into a rectangle about 5 mm/¼ in thick. Cut the remaining lard into little cubes and sprinkle a third of it over the dough, followed by a third of the fruit and a third of the sugar. Then, listen carefully: fold the bottom third of the dough upwards and the top third of the dough downwards and give the whole thing a half turn so you have a vertical rectangle in front of you. Roll this out until you get to a rectangle and repeat the whole process. Then do it again. Once you have incorporated all the lard, sugar and fruit and done the final bit of folding, roll the dough to fit the tin and carefully put it in. Stab it 6–8 times right the way through the dough. Cover with a tea towel and leave to prove in a warm place for 30 minutes.

Preheat the oven to 220°C/425°F/Gas mark 7. Score the top of the cake into 8, if you like, and bake for about 45 minutes or until golden brown. Cool in the tin. If it's difficult to turn out because of all the sticky loveliness in the bottom of the tin, give it a bit of heat and it will release. Smear all the goo back over the lardy. If you are über-greedy (like me) you eat it with butter. In for a penny, in for a pound …

Parkin

I always think of parkin as rather old-fashioned. In my book, old-fashioned combined with cake usually means extremely delicious. This is a real honest, no-frills bake and it's definitely, definitely best eaten a couple of days after you have made it. Accompanying cup of tea non-negotiable.

✳ Serves 16

175 g/6 oz/1 ½ cups plain (all-purpose) flour

350 g/12 oz/4 ¼ cups medium oatmeal

1 tbsp light muscovado sugar

1 tsp ground ginger

450 g/1 lb black treacle

110 g/4 oz/½ cup unsalted butter

75 ml/2 ½ fl oz/scant ⅓ cup milk

1 tsp bicarbonate of soda (baking soda)

Preheat the oven to 180°C/350°F/Gas mark 4. Grease and line a 20 cm/8 in square cake tin (pan). Sift the flour into a large bowl, followed by the oatmeal, sugar and ginger. In a pan, very gently heat the treacle and butter so that they all melt into a glorious mass, then remove from the heat. Warm the milk to hand-hot and add the bicarbonate of soda (baking soda). Then pour both the milk and the treacle and butter mixture into the dry ingredients and gently mix it all together. Don't go hell for leather here – a gentle approach is called for. Tip the mixture into the tin and bake for about 40 minutes or until firm to the touch and a knife or skewer comes out clean.

Cool on a wire rack before cutting into squares and storing in a tin for a few days before eating.

Kouign amann

When I told our friends Colin and Teg about this book they became almost agitated and started behaving in a most unusual manner, muttering about 'Kouign Amann' and making strange slurping noises. Having done some investigation, it now all becomes clear. This is an unashamedly buttery, sugary, caramely cake from Brittany in Northern France. Should there be a faff quota for recipes in this book, it would get five stars. It is, however, worth it. Easy? Not really. Good for you? Absolutely not. Delicious and leave you licking the plate? Yup.

✳ Makes 8 slices

12 g/⅓ oz dried yeast

175 ml/6 fl oz/1 ¼ cups warm water

200 g/7 oz/scant 1 cup caster (superfine) sugar, plus extra for sprinkling

275 g/9 ½ oz/2 ¾ cups strong white bread flour

½ tsp salt

110 g/4 oz/½ cup salted butter, cubed

50 g/1 ¾ oz/scant ¼ cup salted butter, melted

Dissolve the yeast in the water with a pinch of sugar and leave for 15 minutes until foamy.

Put the flour and salt in a large bowl and tip in the yeast mix. Give it a good old stir before tipping it onto a floured work surface and kneading for 10 minutes until smooth and elastic. You may need to regularly flour your hands as this dough is really sticky to start with (more of this later). Put the dough back in the bowl, cover with cling film (plastic wrap) and leave somewhere warm to prove for 1 hour.

Next, cover a large plate with cling film and keep close by. On a lightly floured work surface, roll the dough into a rectangle about 30 x 90 cm/12 x 35 in and have it in 'landscape' form in front of you. This dough sticks, so use a little flour and any implements like spatulas and palette knives to help you if need be.

Imagine that the rectangle of dough is divided into three equal sections and place the cubed butter evenly over the middle section, topped with 50 g/1 ¾ oz/scant ¼ cup sugar. Take the left section of dough, fold it over the butter section and then do the same with the right section. Sprinkle the whole of the top of this long wodge with another 50 g/1 ¾ oz/scant ¼ cup sugar and fold this into thirds so that you end up with a big, fat square of dough. Put it onto the prepared plate and pop it in the fridge for 1 hour.

Take this opportunity to scrape all the gubbins off the work surface and give it a good old clean and dry. This is where your 'extra for sprinkling' sugar comes in: sprinkle a generous amount

onto the worktop. Use it like you would flour for sprinkling. Take the chilled dough out of the fridge and tip it onto the sugared surface. Top the dough with another 50 g/1 ¾ oz/scant ¼ cup sugar and press it in with your fingers before rolling it into a rectangle again, the same size as before. Sprinkle it with yet more sugar and fold it into thirds again, then put it back in the fridge for another hour.

Preheat the oven to 220°C/425°F/Gas mark 7 and liberally grease a 23 cm/9 in cake tin (pan). Take the dough out of the fridge and try to roll it into the same shape as your tin. It's tricky and it might break, in which case deploy the 'patch it in the tin' technique.

Sprinkle the remaining sugar on top of the dough and drizzle with the melted butter. Bake for about 40 minutes or until the top is deeply caramelized, and you can see that it was really worth all the effort. Cool it in the tin for 10 minutes before running a knife round the edge of the tin and carefully transferring to a wire rack.

Bara brith

This is a traditional Welsh tea bread, the name of which translates as 'speckled bread'. There are many versions of this delicious loaf – some use yeast, others self-raising flour. I've gone for the self-raising flour option for the sole reason that it keeps much better. The version made with yeast needs eating that day. This one is simplicity itself and really calls for a good slathering of butter.

✳ Serves 10

450 g/1 lb/2 cups mixed dried fruit

300 ml/10 fl oz/1 ¼ cups tea

2 tbsp marmalade

1 large free-range egg, beaten

6 tbsp light muscovado sugar

1 tsp mixed spice

450 g/1 lb/4 ½ cups self-raising flour

2 tbsp runny honey, to glaze

Soak the fruit overnight in the tea. Next day, preheat the oven to 160°C/325°F/Gas mark 3 and grease and line a 680 g/1 ½ lb loaf tin (pan). Then mix everything apart from the honey in a large bowl and, when it is thoroughly mixed, tip it into the loaf tin. Level the top and bake for about 1 ½ hours. You may need to protect the top of the loaf with greaseproof paper (parchment paper) if it looks as if it is over-browning. It is done when a knife or skewer comes out clean. While the cake is warm, tip it onto a wire rack and brush the top with the runny honey. Leave to cool completely before cutting.

Lavender tea bread

Lavender in a cake isn't as mad as you might think. It's definitely a summery number and really goes well with a dollop of mascarpone cheese and some spanking fresh strawberries. Use lavender that you know hasn't been sprayed with nasty chemicals or by your neighbour's cat. Just wash it, OK? If you can't find lavender, but want something similar, this recipe also works well with other fragrant herbs such as rosemary or lemon balm.

✴ Serves 12

3 tbsp lavender flowers

175 ml/6 fl oz/1 ¼ cups milk

250 g/9 oz/1 cup plus 2 tbsp unsalted butter

175 g/6 oz/¾ cup caster (superfine) sugar

2 large free-range eggs, beaten

350 g/12 oz/3 ½ cups plain (all-purpose) flour

pinch of salt

1 tsp baking powder

Preheat the oven to 160°C/325°F/Gas mark 3. Grease and line a 680 g/1 ½ lb loaf tin (pan). Put the lavender flowers in a small pan with the milk. Gently heat the milk until it barely reaches a simmer, then remove from the heat and let the lavender infuse in the milk for 20 minutes or so.

In a big bowl, cream the butter and sugar until pale and fluffy and then beat in the eggs slowly. Sift half the flour over the mixture together with the salt and baking powder and fold this in. Then carefully fold in half the milk and lavender mixture. Follow this with the second half of the flour and, finally, the remaining milk. Pour the mixture into the tin and bake for about 50 minutes or until a knife or skewer comes out clean. Cool in the tin for about 10 minutes before turning onto a wire rack.

Cheesecakes

OK, it's confession time. For a long time (say, 35 years) I steered well clear of baked cheesecakes. I had an unfortunate incident that resulted in a claggy cheesecake stuck to the roof of my mouth. Interestingly, the first time number one son had some baked cheesecake, his face took on a worried expression, he spat it out and wiped his tongue. That's my boy.

The cheesecake of my early years meant a rather gorgeous affair constructed from three packets that came in a box. I have to say that, although I have managed to move on from those days, a fridge-set cheesecake, albeit made from scratch, is a lovely, lovely thing to eat and extremely quick and easy to make. It's essentially all about stirring a few ingredients in a bowl and tipping it on top of some sort of biscuit base. Bung it in the fridge, and a few hours later you have splendiferous deliciousness.

That, however, is not the end of the story – back to the baked cheesecake. I now adore them – and so does number one son. The key is not to overcook the blighters. They really are hugely versatile; posh pudding or tea-time treat, they can be extravagant or frugal, sweet or savoury, fruity, chocolatey or even fishy! Yes, fishy!

Lots of people avoid cheesecakes, imagining their arteries clogging and thighs expanding as the first morsels pass their lips. May I introduce you to the world of Quark and curd cheese? Virtually fat-free. Yes. It's true. You can use full-fat cream cheese if you like, but nine times out of ten I use Quark, always with magnificent results. All of these recipes work with either full-fat or no-fat cheese – you can even do half and half, if you like. I should point out that there may be a smidge of double (whipping) cream in most of the recipes, which slightly wrecks my argument, but hey, you use Quark, you've halved the fat! May I also point out that it is a cake after all. A cheesecake. A treat. Not everyday food. The only flipside of using Quark is that the texture is slightly grainier, especially in a baked cheesecake – I don't mind it, but if you do, use full-fat.

Anyway, on with the cheesecake show ... it's a good 'un.

The fancy pants cheesecake

The wonderful James (of the Fruit Cake fame, p.76) came for New Year, clutching a cheesecake. It was extremely delicious and, stupidly, I didn't write down his recipe. But remembering the gorgeous combination of banana and Maltesers made me try to replicate it. This is my version of James's original.

✱ Serves 8-10

100 g/3 ½ oz chocolate digestives

100 g/3 ½ oz chocolate Hobnobs

100 g/3 ½ oz/scant ½ cup butter, melted

100 g/3 ½ oz/¾ cup icing (confectioners') sugar, sifted

300 ml/10 fl oz/1 ¼ cups double (whipping) cream

500 g/1 lb 2 oz cream cheese

1 vanilla pod

3 large bananas

juice of 1 lemon

large packet (135 g/4 ¾ oz) of Maltesers

Grease and line a 20 cm/8 in loose-bottomed cake tin (pan). Bash up the biscuits into crumbs, tip them into the melted butter and stir around. Then tip the biscuits into the base of the tin and press down with the back of a spoon so that they are really packed down. Pop the tin in the fridge for an hour.

Add the icing (confectioners') sugar to the cream and whip it until it reaches soft peaks. In another bowl, loosen up the cream cheese by giving it a gentle beating and then fold in the whipped cream. Cut along the length of the vanilla pod, scrape the seeds into the mixture and fold them in.

Slice the bananas and toss them in the lemon juice to stop them browning. Next, put half the cheese mixture on top of the biscuit base and even it out. Place the bananas over the mixture, trying to keep the layer as even as you can. Top with the remaining cheese mixture and smooth the top. Put the whole thing back in the fridge for at least 3 hours.

To serve this beauty, push it out of the tin and remove the base. Peel off the paper and put the cheesecake on a pretty plate. Get those Maltesers and arrange them all over the top. Use milk or white chocolate ones – whatever floats your boat.

Lemon and ricotta baked cheesecake

This a delicious baked cheesecake, devoid of all cloying tendencies and baked without a base. The lemon curd twirlings on the top are purely optional. If you turn to a lemon tart as your default setting for pudding decisions, try this one instead. You'll love it.

✳ Serves 10

750 g/1 lb 10 oz ricotta cheese

175 g/6 oz/¾ cup caster (superfine) sugar

2 tbsp good-quality lemon curd

45 g/1 ½ oz/scant ⅓ cup cornflour (cornstarch)

150 ml/5 fl oz/⅔ cup double (whipping) cream

4 large free-range eggs

300 ml/10 fl oz/1 ¼ cups crème fraîche

2 tsp lemon curd for decoration (optional)

Preheat the oven to 160°C/325°F/Gas mark 3. Grease and line a 20 cm/8 in loose-bottomed cake tin (pan) and then wrap kitchen foil all the way around the base and up the sides.

Beat the ricotta and sugar together until really smooth and then stir in the lemon curd, the cornflour (cornstarch) and the cream. Beat away until it is lovely and smooth and finally add the eggs and give it another quick beat. Pour the mixture into the tin and place it in a roasting tin. Carefully pour warm water into the roasting tin so that it comes halfway up the sides of the cake tin. Bake in the oven for about 1 hour until the cheesecake has set but still has a central wobble to it.

Take the cheesecake out of the oven and remove from the water bath. Spread the crème fraîche over while it's still warm and leave until completely cold. If you wish to, put the lemon curd into a piping (decorating) bag and pipe swirls over the top of the set crème fraîche.

Plain baked cheesecake

Sometimes a very plain version of a cheesecake is just the thing. You may want to have it alongside some form of fruit compote, or simply as an alternative to an egg custard. I love the nutmeg on top here, just giving an old-fashioned, honest flavour to the whole thing. The breadcrumb lining is a very traditional way of baking a baseless cheesecake. I really recommend using full-fat cream cheese here, rather than Quark. You get a smoother texture with the cream cheese, and with this recipe, texture is everything.

✷ Serves 10

25 g/1 oz/1 ¾ tbsp unsalted butter

225 g/8 oz/1 cup caster (superfine) sugar, plus 1 tsp

25 g/1 oz/½ cup white breadcrumbs

700 g/1 lb 8 oz cream cheese

2 large free-range eggs

1 tsp vanilla extract

350 ml/12 fl oz/1 ½ cups double (whipping) cream

40 g/1 ¼ oz/⅓ cup plain (all-purpose) flour

whole nutmeg

Preheat the oven to 160°C/325°F/Gas mark 3. Take all of the butter and smear it evenly over the base and the sides of a 20 cm/8 in tin (pan). Stir 1 teaspoon sugar into the breadcrumbs and press them into the butter as evenly as you can.

Next, mix together the cream cheese, remaining sugar, eggs, vanilla and cream (I use a freestanding mixer, but a wooden spoon followed by a whisk would be fine). Sift the flour over the mixture and fold it in. Pour the mixture into the tin and grate nutmeg all over the top. Bake for about 40–50 minutes or until the cheesecake has set, but still has a wobble in the middle. Cool the cheesecake in the tin, then cover it and pop it in the fridge overnight, or for at least 4 hours. Don't eat it straight from the fridge – reacquaint it with room temperature for about an hour first.

The no-bake vanilla cheesecake

This is a version of the baked vanilla cheesecake for those who cannot or will not eat baked cheesecakes. Interestingly, although they both have very similar ingredients, the taste and the textures are completely different. Curious, but true. Another curiousity is that, unlike the baked version, I think that extra cream doesn't really go, but a bit of fruit does.

✳ Serves 10

200 g/7 oz digestive biscuits, reduced to a crumb

100 g/3 ½ oz/scant ½ cup unsalted butter, melted

3 sheets gelatine

500 g/1 lb 2 oz cream cheese

300 ml/10 fl oz/1 ¼ cups double (whipping) cream

1 vanilla pod

Grease and line a 20 cm/8 in loose-bottomed cake tin (pan). Reduce the biscuits to crumbs, either in a food processor or by bashing them with a rolling pin (put the biscuits in a plastic bag first). Mix the melted butter with the biscuit crumbs. Press the mixture into the bottom of the prepared tin and press down with the back of a spoon. Pop it in the fridge while you get on with the rest.

Put the sheets of gelatine in a shallow dish, cover with cold water and set aside. In a large bowl, beat the cream cheese to loosen it and then stir in the cream. Split the vanilla pod along its length, scrape the seeds into the mixture and stir them in, too.

Take the gelatine out of the water, give it a squeeze and then pop it into a small pan with 2 tablespoons of warm water. Very gently (and I mean very), warm the liquid while stirring until you see the gelatine dissolving. Remove the pan from the heat and keep stirring until it has all dissolved, then quickly whisk it into the cheesecake mixture. Pour everything over the biscuit base in the tin and chill overnight, preferably, or until the cheesecake has set. Serve with lovely summery fruits, or a wintery fruit compote.

Baked vanilla cheesecake

This is sometimes known as a 'New York Cheesecake'. It is big, rich, packed with vanilla and creaminess. It is a bit of a beast, and to be honest, I think that, texturally, it benefits from being baked in a bain marie. This avoids the cloying, roof-of-mouth-sticking episodes that see me running for the hills. The other heavenly thing about this cheesecake is that it is completely acceptable to eat it with extra cream. Yippee!

✳ Serves 12

200 g/7 oz digestive biscuits

100 g/3 ½ oz/scant ½ cup
   unsalted butter, melted

900 g/2 lb cream cheese

175 g/6 oz/¾ cup caster
   (superfine) sugar

4 large free-range eggs

1 vanilla pod

Preheat the oven to 160°C/325°F/Gas mark 3. Grease and line a 20 cm/8 in loose-bottomed deep cake tin (pan) and wrap the whole thing in kitchen foil.

Reduce the biscuits to fine crumbs, either in a food processor or by bashing the living daylights out of them with a rolling pin (put the biscuits in a plastic bag first). Mix the melted butter into the biscuit crumbs, press the sandy mixture into the base of the tin and press down firmly with the back of a spoon. Bung it in the fridge for about 30 minutes.

Then simply beat together the cream cheese, sugar and eggs until you have a smooth mixture. Split the vanilla pod along its length and scrape the seeds into the mixture. Give it a good stir and then pour the mixture over the biscuit base. Put the tin into a roasting tin and pour in enough water to come halfway up the cheesecake tin. Bake for about 1 hour, or until the cheesecake has set but still wobbles in the middle. Take the tin out of the bain marie and leave to cool completely.

Chocolate chip cheesecake

A version of this baked cheesecake appeared in another book of mine, 'Chocolate Magic'. Since I wrote that recipe I have jiggled it a bit, and here is version mark two.

✳ Serves 12

750 g/1 lb 10 oz ricotta cheese

6 large free-range eggs, beaten

200 g/7 oz/ scant 1 cup caster (superfine) sugar

2 tsp vanilla extract

pinch of salt

1 tbsp cocoa

50 g/1 ¾ oz/scant ½ cup plain (all-purpose) flour

100 g/3 ½ oz dark (bittersweet) chocolate, chopped into gravel-sized chunks (or use chocolate chips)

300 ml/10 fl oz/1 ¼ cups sour cream

Preheat the oven to 160°C/325°F/Gas mark 3. Grease and line a 20 cm/8 in loose-bottomed deep cake tin (pan). Beat together the ricotta, eggs, sugar and vanilla, and then sift in the salt, cocoa and flour and mix them in, followed by the chocolate chips. Pour the mixture into the tin and bake for about 1 hour. Check after 45 minutes – you want a slight wobble in the centre of the cheesecake.

Take the cheesecake out of the oven, pour the sour cream over the surface and return the cheesecake to the oven for 5 minutes. Remove from the oven again and leave to cool in the tin.

Rhubarb and ginger cheesecake

Rhubarb and ginger is one of those combinations that people love or loathe. I think it is heaven on a plate. Rhubarb is funny stuff – when it comes, you have a glut of it and seem to be up to your elbows in the stuff. It gets packed into the freezer and lolls around looking forlorn and unloved. This recipe says a big old 'hello!' to frozen rhubarb. It works brilliantly, as long as the pieces haven't been chopped too small – you want distinct pieces of rhubarb as opposed to a mush. The great balls of crystallized (candied) ginger might be a bit much for some, so just slice, sliver or chop as required.

✳ Serves 8–10

100 g/3 ½ oz/scant ½ cup unsalted butter, melted

200 g/7 oz ginger biscuits, crushed

350 g/12 oz/1 ½ cups cream cheese

150 g/5 oz/⅔ cup caster (superfine) sugar

4 large free-range eggs, lightly beaten

300 g/10 oz cooked rhubarb

1 jar (190 g/6 ¾ oz) crystallized (candied) ginger in syrup

Grease and line a 20 cm/8 in loose-bottomed deep cake tin (pan) and wrap it in kitchen foil. Preheat the oven to 160°C/325°F/Gas mark 3. Mix the melted butter into the ginger biscuits and tip the lot into the bottom of the tin. Press it down well with the back of a spoon and pop it in the fridge to harden.

In a big bowl, beat the cream cheese to soften and loosen it and add the sugar and eggs. Give it all a jolly good beat. Then carefully fold in the rhubarb, trying not to break up the pieces of rhubarb too much. Taste the mixture to check for sweetness and add more sugar if you need to.

Pour the mixture on top of the biscuit base and transfer the tin to a roasting dish. Fill with enough water to come halfway up the sides of the cake tin and bake for about 30 minutes. The cheesecake is done when it has set, but the centre still wobbles a bit.

Remove the cheesecake from the bain marie and, when it is cold, spoon the crystallized (candied) ginger and a small amount of the syrup over the top of the cheesecake.

Gooseberry and elderflower cheesecake

Gooseberries and elderflowers are two flavours that adore each other. As a combination, they taste of early summer. How is this possible, I hear you cry? Well, you try this and tell me it doesn't taste of early summer.

✳ Serves 8–10

For the pastry:

175 g/6 oz/¾ cup unsalted butter

50 g/1 ¾ oz/scant ¼ cup caster (superfine) sugar

250 g/9 oz/2 ½ cups plain (all-purpose) flour

1 large free-range egg yolk

1 tbsp very cold water

For the filling:

4 sheets gelatine

300 ml/10 fl oz/1 ¼ cups double (whipping) cream

250 g/9 oz/1 cup ricotta cheese

150 g/5 oz cooked gooseberries and 100 ml/3 ½ fl oz/scant ½ cup of their cooking juices

2 tbsp elderflower cordial

juice of ½ lemon

For the glaze:

3 tbsp gooseberry jam

2 tbsp elderflower cordial

juice of ½ lemon

First make the pastry by creaming together the butter and the sugar. Add 1 tablespoon of the flour and beat this in, followed by the egg yolk. Beat in the rest of the flour a spoonful at a time and then finally add just enough water to bring the pastry together into a ball. Turn it out onto a lightly floured surface and knead it a couple of times before wrapping it in cling film (plastic wrap) and chilling in the fridge for at least 1 hour – 2 would be better.

After the allotted chilling time, grease a 24 cm/9 ½ in pie dish (or flan dish if you prefer). Roll out the pastry to about 2 mm/⅛ in thick and line the dish, leaving a good overhang of pastry. Prick it all over with a fork and pop it back in the fridge for 30 minutes.

Preheat the oven to 190°C/375°F/Gas mark 5 and place a baking sheet in the oven to heat up. Take the pastry case out of the fridge, place greaseproof paper (parchment paper) on top and weigh it down with baking beans or dry rice. Bake for 15 minutes, then remove the beans and paper and return the pastry case to the oven for another 5 minutes or so until thoroughly cooked and golden brown. Leave to cool before trimming the edges off.

While the case is cooling, soak the gelatine in a shallow dish with some water. Whip the cream until it forms soft peaks and set aside. In another bowl, beat the ricotta until smooth and then fold in the whipped cream and the gooseberries. In a small pan, very gently heat the elderflower cordial, lemon juice and gooseberry cooking juices. Squeeze out the water from the gelatine, add the gelatine to the pan of warm liquid and stir until it has all dissolved. Then quickly mix the liquid into the cheesecake mixture, ensuring that it is all thoroughly incorporated. Tip the filling into the cold pastry case and level the surface. Pop it in the fridge until it has set (1–2 hours).

To make the glaze, warm the jam with the cordial and lemon juice and taste. Add more cordial or lemon if you need to. Push the mixture through a fine sieve and pour over the set cake. Return to the fridge for at least 1 hour for the glaze to set.

Apricot swirl cheesecake in a chocolate shell

Now, doesn't this look impressive? It's an absolute cinch. Really. Don't tell anyone. Please pretend it's difficult. Let's keep our egos intact, shall we?

✳ Serves 10

dash of sunflower oil

200 g/7 oz dark (bittersweet) chocolate (at least 70% cocoa solids), broken into chunks

25 g/1 oz/1 ¾ tbsp unsalted butter, cubed

1 can (350 g/10 ½ oz) apricots in fruit juice, drained

325 g/11 oz/1 ⅓ cups cream cheese

2 tbsp icing (confectioners') sugar, sifted

zest and juice of 1 lime

300 ml/10 fl oz/1 ¼ cups double (whipping) cream, whipped

To make the chocolate shell, grease and line a loose-bottomed 20 cm/8 in cake tin (pan). Then brush the inside of the greaseproof paper (parchment paper) with a little sunflower oil. Place a heatproof bowl over a pan of barely simmering water, ensuring that the base of the bowl doesn't touch the water. Put the chocolate and butter into the bowl and let them gently melt together.

When the chocolate has melted, stir it all gently to make a shiny emulsion and then tip the whole lot into the bottom of the prepared tin. Now start rocking and rolling the tin gently so that the chocolate moves all over the base and rolls round the sides of the tin. As it cools, the mixture thickens and you get more of a feel for it building up a wall of chocolate. Then put the tin in the fridge for the chocolate to set.

In a liquidizer or with a hand blender, blitz the apricots then push the purée through a sieve to make as smooth a sauce as you can. Set aside.

Beat the cream cheese with the icing (confectioners') sugar for a few moments to soften and then fold in the lime juice and zest followed by the double (whipping) cream.

Take the chocolate-lined tin out of the fridge and place alternate spoons of apricot purée and cheesecake mix into it. Build up several layers until you run out of cheesecake mixture (you will have some apricot left over – don't panic). To create the swirls you need to carefully mix the two sets of ingredients. I find a chopstick the perfect tool for the job. Don't over-swirl or it will all mix into one mush. Less is more here. Put the finished article back in the fridge for a few hours to firm up.

It is super-easy to get out of the tin and away from the paper, thanks to the oiling procedure, but it doesn't care, very much, for hanging around in warm rooms for hours on end. Serve with the left-over apricot coulis.

Rocky road cheesecake

Rocky Road is a form of confection that I can't get enough of. I made a Rocky Road Cookie once. It was lovely. So, of course, not to let the side down, I decided to make a Rocky Road Cheesecake. A triumph, though I say so myself. Not sophisticated, but fairly spectacular in a gluttony kind of way. I made a slightly smaller cheesecake than normal here, but it's so sweet and rich that a small amount really does go a long way.

✳ Serves 12

50 g/1 ¾ oz/scant ¼ cup unsalted butter

1 ½ tbsp golden syrup

100 g/3 ½ oz dark (bittersweet) chocolate (at least 70% cocoa solids), broken into chunks

50 g/1 ¾ oz milk chocolate, broken into chunks

125 g/4 ½ oz digestive biscuits, broken into large chunks

50 g/1 ¾ oz/1 cup marshmallows

50 g/1 ¾ oz/scant ½ cup hazelnuts, whole

250 g/9 oz/1 cup cream cheese

300 ml/10 fl oz/1 ¼ cups double (whipping) cream, whipped

1 tbsp icing (confectioners') sugar, sifted

1 tsp vanilla extract

marshmallows, biscuits, hazelnuts and chocolate to decorate (optional)

First, grease and line a deep 18 cm/7 in loose-bottomed cake tin (pan). Set a heatproof bowl over barely simmering water (making sure the bottom of the bowl doesn't touch the water), add the butter, syrup and dark and milk chocolate and leave to slowly melt and ooze into a goo of such wonder that you will want to submerge your face in it. Please don't, but you may stir it gently.

Put the biscuit rubble, marshmallows and hazelnuts in a larger bowl, then pour the chocolate sauce over them. Stir it all together, plonk it into the bottom of the tin and press it down well. Put the tin in the fridge and try not to pick at it.

Next, beat the cream cheese until smooth and then fold in the whipped cream, the icing (confectioners') sugar and the vanilla. When the base has hardened, spoon the cheesecake mixture on top, level the surface and then place back into the fridge for at least 4 hours.

If you are feeling particularly greedy (I always do), top the cheesecake with a few more marshmallows, bits of broken biscuit and hazelnuts and pour over some melted chocolate, or, if you can be bothered, make another small amount of the sauce with the butter and the syrup, too.

Baked raspberry cheesecake

Lovely, lovely, lovely. And equally good made with frozen raspberries. You could make this with blueberries or blackberries, too.

* Serves 10

100 g/3 ½ oz/scant ½ cup unsalted butter, melted

100 g/3 ½ oz chocolate digestives, crushed to crumbs

100 g/3 ½ oz ginger biscuits, crushed to crumbs

900 g/2 lb cream cheese

175 g/6 oz/¾ cup caster (superfine) sugar

4 large free-range eggs, lightly beaten

150 g/5 oz/1 cup raspberries

Preheat the oven to 160°C/325°F/Gas mark 3. Grease and line a 20 cm/8 in cake tin (pan) and then wrap it in kitchen foil.

Pour the melted butter over the biscuit crumbs and stir to make a sandy mixture. Tip into the tin, press down with the back of a spoon and pop the tin in the fridge to firm up.

Beat the cream cheese and caster (superfine) sugar together and then beat in the eggs. Distribute the mixture on top of the biscuit base, then pop the raspberries on top and push them down slightly so you feel they are distributed evenly throughout the cheesecake.

Put the tin into a roasting tin and pour in enough water to come halfway up the cake tin. Bake for about 45 minutes or until the cheesecake is set, but still has a good wobble in the middle. Take the tin out of the bain marie and leave to cool.

Easy cheesecake pots

This is one of those mildly embarrassing recipes, because it's so simple. The truth is, though, that it's a lovely pudding. It looks pretty, and has all the components required in a cheesecake. It just happens to take 5 minutes to make about 8 of them.

✳ Makes 8

100 g/3 ½ oz/scant ½ cup
unsalted butter, melted

100 g/3 ½ oz digestive biscuits,
crushed

100 g/3 ½ oz oaty biscuits such
as Hobnobs, crushed

750 g/10 oz/3 ⅓ cups
mascarpone cheese

about 6 tbsp runny honey

400 g/14 oz/2 ¾ cups
blueberries

Mix the melted butter with the crushed biscuits and then put a heaped teaspoonful in the bottom of 8 pudding glasses or bowls. Place a spoonful of mascarpone on top of the biscuits, followed by a drizzle of honey and a scattering of blueberries. Keep going in this manner until you have filled the glasses and there's a layer of blueberries on top. That's it. I told you it was easy.

Amaretto cheesecake with an amaretti base

This no-cook cheesecake involves two of my favourite things: amaretto liqueur and Amaretti biscuits. I can only make it occasionally because my will-power is so non-existent that I have been known to take the odd Amaretti biscuit, dip it in the amaretto liqueur and eat it quite happily instead of actually using the ingredients in the proper manner. I then wonder why my head is spinning and I am running low on biscuits and liquid. By that stage, I don't really care and wander off without making a cheesecake at all.

✳ Serves 12

100 g/3 ½ oz/1 cup toasted flaked almonds

100 g/3 ½ oz/scant ½ cup unsalted butter, melted

200 g/7 oz Amaretti biscuits, crushed

350 g/12 oz/1 ½ cups cream cheese

1 tbsp icing (confectioners') sugar, sifted

300 ml/10 fl oz/1 ¼ cups double (whipping) cream, whipped

2–3 tbsp amaretto liqueur

100 g/3 ½ oz Amaretti biscuits

Grease and line a 20 cm/8 in loose-bottomed cake tin (pan). Roughly chop half the almonds. Pour the melted butter over the crushed biscuits and stir in the chopped almonds. Mix everything together, put into the baking tin and press down with the back of a spoon. Put the tin in the fridge.

Beat the cream cheese and icing (confectioners') sugar until smooth and then fold in the whipped cream and the amaretto. Taste it to make sure you have enough sugar and liqueur. I know, dangerous ... When you are happy, tip the mixture into the tin, smooth it out and put it back in the fridge for 2 hours. When you are ready to serve the cheesecake, remove it from the tin and peel off the paper. Top the cheesecake with the whole Amaretti biscuits and scatter the remaining toasted almonds over the top, too.

Coconut and lime cheesecake loaf

Where does it say that cheesecakes need to be round? Nowhere, that's where. This is a sort of upside-down system of making a cheesecake, but when you turn it out, hey presto, it all comes right. This would be a great pudding after a spicy meal. It's cooling and palate-cleansing and just the thing after a threatening vindaloo.

✳ Serves 10–12

4 sheets gelatine

350 g/12 oz/1 ½ cups cream cheese

400 ml/14 fl oz/1 ¾ cups coconut milk

1 tbsp icing (confectioners') sugar, sifted

zest and juice of 2 limes

100 g/3 ½ oz/scant ½ cup unsalted butter

200 g/7 oz oaty biscuits such as Hobnobs, crushed to crumbs

1 lime, to garnish (optional)

First, line a 1 kg/2 lb loaf tin (pan) with two layers of cling film (plastic wrap). Put the gelatine in a shallow dish, cover with cold water and leave to soak.

In a large bowl, beat together the cream cheese, coconut milk, icing (confectioners') sugar and lime zest and set aside. In a small pan, heat the lime juice. Squeeze the water out of the gelatine and add it to the warm lime juice, stirring constantly, removing the pan from the heat as soon as the gelatine looks as if it's dissolving. Once it has all dissolved, quickly whisk it into the cheesecake mixture and pour it into the prepared tin. Put the tin in the fridge and leave for 2 hours to set.

Once the cheesecake has set, make the biscuit 'base' by melting the butter and stirring it into the biscuit crumbs. Then tip the mixture carefully over the surface of the set cheesecake and return it to the fridge for another 2 hours.

When you are ready to serve the pudding, remove the cheesecake out of the fridge and turn the tin onto a plate, easing it away from the cling film. You can then simply peel the cling film off and there you have it – a cheesecake loaf with a biscuit base. Slice another lime thinly and lay the slices on top of the cheesecake.

Very cheesy cheesecakes

I liked the idea of having little savoury cheesecakes as a light lunch or a starter – something that could be eaten with a spoon, with a bit of salad on the side – and so the Very Cheesy Cheesecake was born. I must say that these are definitely best eaten barely warm rather than completely cold. They lose their inner goo once they have cooled completely and also have a tendency to sink slightly. Not a horror, but they are better just warm. The cheeses used are very swappable – you need the cream cheese, but feel free to substitute blue cheeses or other strong, hard cheeses.

✳ Makes 8

100 g/3 ½ oz/scant ½ cup unsalted butter, melted, plus extra for greasing

200 g/7 oz Ritz crackers, or similar, crushed

350 g/12 oz/1 ½ cups cream cheese

4 large free-range eggs, lightly beaten

150 g/5 oz parmesan cheese, grated

150 g/5 oz strong cheddar cheese, grated

1 tsp mustard powder

2 tbsp double (whipping) cream

salt and pepper

Preheat the oven to 150°C/300°F/Gas mark 2. Butter 8 ramekins and set to one side. Mix the melted butter with the crushed biscuits and divide between the ramekins, pressing down firmly with the back of a spoon.

Beat together the cream cheese, eggs, parmesan, cheddar, mustard powder and cream and season to taste with salt and pepper. Pour the mixture into the ramekins and place them in a roasting tin (pan). Pour enough water into the tin to reach the halfway point on the ramekins and bake for about 20 minutes or until just set but still with a wobble in the middle.

Take the pots out of the bain marie and leave for 15 minutes or so before serving.

Salmon and dill cheesecake

This is just the job for a summer lunch party. You can make a big one and slice it or go for little individual ones. It is very fresh and light, and an absolute doddle to make.

✳ Serves 8–10

For the pastry:

110 g/4 oz/½ cup unsalted butter

225 g/8 oz/2 cups plain (all-purpose) flour

pinch of salt

2 large free-range egg yolks

For the filling:

200 g/7 oz smoked salmon

250 g/9 oz/scant 1 ¼ cups mascarpone cheese

250 g/9 oz/1 cup ricotta

1 tbsp fresh dill, chopped

juice of 1 lemon

salt and pepper

Start by making the pastry. Rub the butter into the flour until the mixture resembles breadcrumbs. Add the salt and stir in the egg yolks. Add just enough very cold water to bring everything together to form a dough. I use my hands for this – much easier than messing around with a spoon. Alternatively, bung it all in the food processor. Wrap the pastry in cling film (plastic wrap) and leave it in the fridge for at least 1 hour.

After the pastry has chilled, grease and flour a 25 cm/10 in diameter dish (metal always works best) and preheat the oven to 200°C/400°F/Gas mark 6. On a lightly floured surface, roll out the pastry to about 3 mm/⅛ in thick and line the tin (pan) with it, leaving a good overhang of pastry. Prick the bottom with a fork and bung it back in the fridge for 30 minutes. Five minutes before you get the pastry case out of the fridge, put a baking tray in the oven to heat up. Put the pastry case directly onto the hot sheet and bake for 20 minutes or so, until it is cooked through and golden brown. Remove the pastry from the oven, trim all the untidy edges and leave to cool.

To make the filling, chop the salmon into strips about 5 mm/¼ in wide. Beat together the mascarpone and the ricotta. Add the dill, the chopped salmon and some of the lemon juice. Taste the mixture and see how much more lemon you think it needs and whether a bit of salt and pepper would perk the whole thing up (I find it usually does). When you are happy with the seasoning, put the mixture into the pastry case and even it out. Put the whole thing back in the fridge for 1–2 hours to firm up. Serve at room temperature with extra lemon, a smattering of salad leaves and a glass of something cold and white.

Feta, mint and spinach cheesecakes

Every book I write seems to have at least one recipe that challenges (quite radically) the essence of the chapter. This cheesecake is such a recipe. Before you get cross, what exactly is a cheesecake? We have ascertained that it can be sweet or savoury and they all seem to contain cream cheese. Well, this recipe is savoury and contains cream cheese – its largest component, by far. Therefore, it must be a cheesecake. I won't tell you what my husband called it (while happily eating it, may I add), but it certainly wasn't cheesecake. Call it what you will, it is utterly delicious. Will that do?

✳ Makes 6 individual
   cheesecakes

250 g/9 oz spinach

250 g/9 oz/1 cup ricotta cheese

250 g/9 oz/scant 1 ¼ cups
   mascarpone cheese

1 tbsp fresh dill, chopped

1 tbsp fresh mint, chopped

3 large free-range eggs,
   lightly beaten

200 g/7 oz/about 1 ¾ cups
   feta cheese

salt and pepper

125 g/4 ½ oz/½ cup
   plus 1 tbsp unsalted
   butter, melted

1 packet (270 g/9 ½ oz) filo
   pastry

Cook the spinach in 1 tablespoon of water, wilting it right down. Put it in a sieve over a bowl and let the fluid drain out. When the spinach is cold, push and squeeze as much fluid out of it as you possibly can and then chop it up.

Preheat the oven to 180°C/350°F/Gas mark 4. In a large bowl, combine the ricotta and mascarpone and mix in the herbs, spinach and eggs. Crumble the feta into the mix and stir it in. Add salt and pepper to taste – be careful with the salt, as feta can be really salty.

Grease the individual pie tins (pans) with some of the melted butter. Take the filo pastry out of its wrapping and cut the whole lot in half. Take one piece and push it into a pie tin in quite a haphazard manner – it will overhang the edge and look a bit of a state. Brush with butter and continue this layering approach until you have 4–6 layers of pastry and the bottom and the side of the tin are covered evenly, although quite untidily. You need this messy look to get the really lovely crispy texture in the pastry.

Repeat with all the pie tins and then spoon in the cheesy mixture. Bake for 15–20 minutes or until the pastry is golden and the centre has just set. Eat hot, warm or cold. Definitely a cheesecake. Probably.

Gorgonzola and pear cheesecake with walnuts

I have always loved starters that involve little salads of blue cheese and something a little bit sweet to offset the sharpness of the cheese – it might be honey, or nuts or fruit. Gorgonzola and pear are a classic combination and I thought they would go well in a cheesecake that you could have as a starter or even a cheese course. The result was good, but lacking something – it really needs the crunch of the walnuts with their salty, sweet coating. An accompanying few slices of poached pear and a little salad with a delicious dressing and the job is done. This is a very rich cheesecake and a little goes a long way.

1 litre/1 ¾ pt water

2 tbsp caster (superfine) sugar

juice of 1 lemon

4 pears (any variety and
    they don't need to be
    completely ripe)

150 g/5 oz/⅔ cup unsalted
    butter, melted

150 g/5 oz Ritz crackers, or
    similar, crushed

150 g/5 oz oatcakes, crushed

350 g/12 oz/1 ½ cups
    cream cheese

125 g/4 ½ oz/1 cup
    gorgonzola cheese

4 large free-range eggs

100 g/3 ½ oz/scant ½ cup
    unsalted butter

150 g/5 oz/1 ¼ cups walnuts

2 tbsp caster (superfine) sugar

1 tbsp light muscovado sugar

1 tsp sea salt flakes such
    as Maldon

Put the water, sugar and lemon juice in a big saucepan and get the heat going under it. Meanwhile, peel the pears, leaving them whole and immediately dropping each one into the pan to stop it browning. Bring the pears up to simmering point and simmer them until they are soft – how long very much depends on the size of the pears and how ripe or unripe they are. The tip of a sharp knife easily slides in when they are done. Take the pan off the heat and leave the pears in the syrup.

Next, make the base for the cheesecake by stirring the melted butter into the crackers and oatcakes. Grease and line a 20 cm/8 in square cake tin (pan). Provide really high sides of greaseproof paper (parchment paper) as this gives you something to tug on when you want to get the cheesecake out of the tin in one piece. Put the biscuit mixture into the bottom of the tin, press it down with the back of a spoon and stick it in the fridge for about 30 minutes to harden.

Preheat the oven to 150°C/300°F/Gas mark 2. Take two pears out of the syrup, core them and chop them into 1 cm/½ in cubes. Mix the cream cheese and gorgonzola together and beat in the eggs. Finally, stir in the chopped pear. Pour the mixture onto the biscuit base and put the tin in a roasting dish half full of water. Cook for about 30 minutes, or until the top of the cheesecake has set and there is a slight wobble to the middle. Take the tin out of the bain marie and leave to cool completely. When the cheesecake is cold, use the lining to haul it out of the tin and then cut it into squares.

To make the salty, sweet walnuts, melt the butter in a frying pan and throw in the walnuts followed by both types of sugar. Stir everything around for about 5 minutes until the nuts are covered with a sweet, sugary sort of rubble, but don't let the sugar melt completely – you don't want caramel. Finally, add the salt and give everything a good stir. Have a taste and check whether you need to add more salt. Tip all the nuts and sugary, salty remnants onto a sheet of silicone paper and leave to cool.

To serve the cheesecake, sprinkle some nuts over each square and add a few slices of poached pear. A little salad with a balsamic type of dressing is just perfect.

Index

Acknowledgements

Writing a book about cake sounds like one big party, but I have to say that I really couldn't have done it without help from some really special people. There were those who were incredibly generous with their recipes and advice: Lady Helene, Gretchen, Claire, Tony Manley of Shepherd's in Chieveley and James-the-Cake Woodhead all deserve special mentions. Lady Helene (actually Helen) deserves huge thanks for putting up with me, constantly wading through the chaos and sorting it out, only to re-encounter it time after time. Her sorting-out skills are legendary and I honestly don't know how she does it. She is not only a great colleague, but a true friend. Plus, she bakes a mighty lemon drizzle ...

Thank you to all at Pavilion and Anova Books for believing in me enough to ask me to write another book. Special thanks to Nina and Georgie.

Thank you to Jenniflower in Exeter for lending me lovely china, and Charlotte Barton who has the craziest selection of prop gems I have ever seen. It was quite hard to give them back.

To my beautiful models: Rory, Toby, Jack, Chris and April – thanks for eating so much cake. It's a hard job, I know.

Emma Solley has been a complete joy to work with. As a photographer she produces the most beautiful images with such good humour and unflappability, sometimes in the face of adversity. Thank you, Ems, and I am sorry I trashed your studio time after time. I would also like to extend my thanks to the family of Emma – the Chatterjees, who have all helped out at one point or another.

Finally, thank you to Tarek and Rory who, as usual, have had to put up with me muttering about cake and nothing else for some months. Thank you, my lovely chaps.